M000115001

Star Rating: 4.5/5

"What do you do when you can't find a book that addresses the issues you want to hear about? You write it! Author Andrea R. Huff's book *Every Night's Friday Night* is a book about the third stage of a person's life when they are about to retire. A fascinating group of people was selected to be interviewed about how they prepared (or didn't prepare) to retire and the tips they would give others who are retiring.

Huff gives the reader several resources so that he or she can research the suggestions given by herself and her interviewees. I found this book to be extremely informative. A book for all ages, even those who are not in the third stage yet."

San Francisco Book Review

5.0

*****

"Andrea R. Huff has created a wonderful book, *Every Night's Friday Night*, that is relatable, compassionate and easy to read. There is a levity to Huff's writing that made me instantly at ease with the subject matter, furnishing real life stories, examples and exercises at the end of each chapter. I loved this book and all it had to offer!

I would recommend this book to coaches, counselors, retirement planners, and to those in, considering or who have someone they care about entering the third stage of their lives."

Readers' Favorite

Every Night's Friday Night

Time and Freedom
For the Rest of Your Life

Andrea R. Huff

Dedicated to my husband, Michael,
our son, Jeffrey,
daughter-in-law, Leah
and grandson, Max.

I'm grateful for their love and support.

They put meaning and fun in my life.

Contents

Introduction   1

Chapter 1 – Time for Transformation   19

Chapter 2 – Design Thinking Creates
Your Third Stage Identity   31

Chapter 3 – Paradox Thinking Expands
Your Options   43

Chapter 4 – Change and Adversity
Can Be an Advantage   55

Chapter 5 – Body, Brain, and Pain   69

Chapter 6 – An Inner Journey of Mindfulness
and Spirituality   87

Chapter 7 – Connections to Others   97

Chapter 8 – Time Is the New Money   105

Chapter 9 – Creative Growth Activities   119

Chapter 10 – Your Legacy and Completion of Life   125

Summary   133

Epilogue   139

Acknowledgments   145

Ways to Contact Me   147

Bibliography   149

Author Bio   153

Introduction

Today is the beginning of the unknown. Yesterday was my last day of work at a company where I held six different jobs in 24 years. Now I'm free, my time is my own, and I face my biggest challenge. Where do I find purpose, meaning, and fulfillment now that I don't have the validation of an organization and a team of people to collaborate with? That door has closed, and a new one will open the next stage of my life. Now I just need to find the key!

I know I'm not alone in this feeling. I talk to many people struggling with this challenge. They tell me they had satisfying careers, or at least jobs to go to, and now they no longer have them to rely on for a large part of their identity and purpose. Like me, they feel empowered and free, but some are experiencing loss also. This can be a good problem to have, and yet its solution requires a major mind shift and a new structure to make aging and retirement one of the best times of life. Facing it now, I realize retirement is one of life's major transitions, yet most people receive no help in making this shift from looking outside themselves for meaning and structure to creating these internally.

I want to clarify that when I use the word *retirement* in this book, I don't mean "not working." In many cases, people still do some type of work part time or full time, by choice or need during what I call this third stage of life after age 60 or when we are no longer working full time. Most people today are looking for an active retirement, and many in this stage of life become entrepreneurs.

It's time to disrupt the negative view our culture has of retirement and aging as a diminishing period. Instead, we must celebrate this stage of life as the most fulfilling and impactful.

I don't have a problem with the word *retirement*, even though I've heard many people say they don't want to use the word because of the negative connotations. I'd rather redefine the concept of retirement because the problem is not the word, but how the culture interprets it, and how others respond to someone who has retired from a full-time role, or is in the third stage of life.

The Stages of Life

Each stage of life is fascinating and challenging. The first stage of life I'll define as learning, which happens most intensely in the first 30 years, although hopefully we continue to learn throughout our lives.

The second is the stage of achievement from your 30s to your 60s, when you grow a career, possibly a family, and establish your expertise.

The third stage of life begins at whatever age you are when you quit working full time or taking directions from others, and shift to find your own path for the remainder of your life. This stage is dedicated to personal fulfillment and inner development and generally begins at age 60-plus, although some people start earlier. Within this stage, your focus may be different if you are at the beginning of this stage (60 to 80) than if you are at the later part of the stage (80-plus). These years of the third stage are not a time to sit back and do little with the remaining time left, but rather to make these the most satisfying and meaningful years of your life. If others observe us doing this, they can change their thinking about what retirement and aging holds for them. We want to transform aging, not adapt to it. The sooner we stop fearing growing older, the sooner we can take advantage of the many ways it can be enriching.

The third stage of life is often viewed by many in our society as a period of decline. I hold the opposite view. I think it can be the period of greatest expansion and growth. A time to do your best work. A phase in life that brings joy and offers time and freedom to try new things, which until now have been scarce commodities for most people.

Even as physical aspects of our body change and may introduce new challenges, there are other parts of life that can become more satisfying. I know many people who are healthier and in better physical shape in their 70s than they were in their 40s.

This is a time to be visible and out in the world modeling for others an active, satisfying aging process. It's a time to enjoy children, grandchildren, and friends. It's also a time to work with others who share your purpose to create change and add value to the world. It's a time to do whatever you choose to do, and to be a *perennial*, as Gina Pell from Thewhatlist.com defines as curious people of all ages who have a mindset of learning, who defy stereotypes, and who never let their age limit their behavior, interests, or social groups.

I don't want to sound overly optimistic in this book. Aging can be a challenging time of life due to illness, loss of friends and family, and financial concerns, but there are ways to not only overcome these difficulties, but use them to our advantage to create new options.

Adversity can create opportunity if we have the internal wisdom and fortitude to endure what life serves up to us. These difficulties give us material to work with to learn life's lessons and trust our inner selves. Granted, we often aren't looking for material to work with—it's going to find us anyway—so we might as well do something productive with it.

A Roadmap for the Transition

A problem many people face is they don't have a road-map showing how to move down this path from the second stage of life focused on external accomplishment, to the third stage of life driven by inner development and purpose. There's something satisfying about having a routine, a place to go, and people who expect you to be there, even if these people and places aren't ideal. They still provide a structure and process to let us know we belong somewhere outside our homes, and we should be doing something other than spending time on our phones, computers, or checking out what's on TV.

Human beings like having a purpose. Where do we start when that purpose is removed, even if it was one we weren't crazy about to begin with? Some people are very self-motivated and can create many satisfying and fulfilling activities that bring meaning to their lives. However, from the discussions I've had with many people, including my clients, it's a smaller percent of people who know how to create this purpose and meaning on their own. What about the people who are not as internally driven or who need help cultivating that part of them long dormant?

Many people are used to responding to stimulation from other people and places, and are not practiced at creating their own activities that aren't busywork or leisure, but that bring them long-term fulfillment, and cause them to feel they're reaching their potential and destiny.

Transitioning to retirement can be harder for people whose work was their primary identity. This requires a new mindset that resonates with us as our true selves, which may be different from the identity that served us well in the second stage of life when we were working. The third stage of life can often be the last 30-plus years of our lives, if we are fortunate. This is a long period of time to spend doing things that don't bring satisfaction or a sense of purpose.

This time in life is complex, and can bring many distractions to finding your sense of identity and fulfillment—health issues, financial issues, responsibilities for aging parents, children who have returned home, and other issues that require time, attention, and money. There's no lack of obstacles that come up when you least expect them. After a lifetime of feeling healthy, I've been dealing with chronic pain and two surgeries during the last five years. This has been a total surprise for me, and a distraction in preparing for retirement.

I've been trying to plan my retirement from a full-time, all-encompassing job I loved, one that allowed me to end my corporate career doing work that felt like it made a difference. But, pain has a way of making it hard to identify creative options and contributions to our communities, to leave legacies for others and find fulfillment for ourselves when it's hard to even get out of bed. It's all you can do to maintain the job you have without thinking about what comes next.

However, I've learned (the hard way) that pain can be a guidepost for what needs to happen next for us. Pain lets us know that our body/mind needs more care. Pain can be a great motivator to move beyond it to a different awareness of increased focus and creativity.

Pain can also give us compassion for the struggles of others. People who've always been healthy generally don't have this understanding because they haven't experienced living with chronic pain. It can be a heart-opening experience.

Quit as Soon as You Can

Many people prepare for this third stage of life by seeing a financial planner or accountant to invest their money, or determine if the amount they have is enough to quit working.

My approach throughout this book is based on the premise that time is the new money, and it's equally important to spend it well. Just as it's critical to invest your money in a diversified way, it's also critical to find a combination of activities to provide meaning, stretch your thinking, force you to learn new things, focus on a purpose you're passionate about, and develop your inner life. Many people are concerned about achieving a certain level of savings and investments before it's time to retire. They have an artificial number in their heads about how much is enough, or have been given an inflated number from a financial advisor. However, I'm finding people can live well on less than they thought, and can continue earning some money in new ventures long after they retire from full-time work. A study done by Pew Research Center in 2006 found that 77 percent of workers expect to work at least part time for money after retirement.

However, if you wait too long to retire, the thing you won't have enough of is time. Time is the thing you can't make more of. If you or your partner or friends suddenly become ill, the time you planned to spend together won't be there in the same way. The time you hoped you'd have to do the things you always wanted to get around to, can quickly become short. Don't wait too long to step out of a job if you can afford to, even if you've been happy with it. Give yourself time to explore the identity you want at this stage, and to pursue the things you'd like to do before it's too late.

It's important to have an abundance mindset, not a scarcity mindset when approaching this stage of life. This may sound like a paradox, that you could feel abundance while encountering a scarcity of time, but I believe paradox thinking produces the most creative options at this stage, or in any stage, of life. I've devoted a chapter to paradox thinking in this book.

I find some people intuitively know when it's time to leave their jobs or businesses, and if they have the resources they trust new opportunities will present themselves, if they are open to them.

I've been an executive and business coach, leadership consultant, career consultant, and managing director of a region for a global career management and leadership development company. I've been doing consulting work my entire career, helping people find their next positions, ideal career paths, and growing their own businesses. I've led large teams of people, and have delivered consulting services myself.

Yet, I find consulting with people entering the third stage of their lives, as I am now, requires a broader view and a more holistic and complex process. There's no clear-cut way to prepare your resume, use social media, and go on interviews to find the purpose and fulfillment you desire at this stage. This can only come internally from you, perhaps with the help of a coach, counselor, or friend. No one prepares you for the changes you'll need to initiate yourself if you want to make this the best time of your life. Some people are very change averse and don't seek new things willingly. This makes the third stage much more difficult because it's inevitable you will experience more changes during this period than at any previous time in your life.

I hope to disrupt the thinking you may have about change being something to fear by helping you become more comfortable with change as a positive force, and to give you a process and the resources to help you create the purpose you desire during this stage. I want you to experience the fact that aging equals freedom.

For the last several years, I've been preparing for the time when I would leave my full-time corporate job and enter this third stage of life. I thought I was prepared, but it was more difficult than I expected. There were many questions I needed to address both individually and with my husband that we had not discussed before.

In going through this myself, I created a process that worked for us, and I've been using it with clients I see in my consulting firm, Third Stage of Life Consulting, to help them make this transition. The chapters and exercises in this book describe the approach I took, and the different questions that needed to be answered, and I'm hopeful this process can be useful to you as well. I also do entrepreneurial consulting with many of my clients. If you are already an entrepreneur, in the third stage you may want to scale your business more aggressively, reduce the time you spend on certain aspects of the business, change the focus of it, or sell it.

Many of my clients are becoming entrepreneurs for the first time in the third stage of life by starting businesses, consulting firms, or doing totally different work than they've done in the past. This pool of senior entrepreneurial talent will be large and beneficial to our communities.

The third stage of life is also beginning earlier for many people than it did in the past. I have people contacting me who are 50 who want to create a new identity and forge a meaningful way to enter this third stage. They want to start planning for it now, and some are ready to start living it now. Some partners at large consulting firms are required to retire at an early age so they have an even larger number of years to begin a totally new career, if they choose. Even if they are searching for a new full-time job or are starting or expanding a business, they want to transition well as they age.

People in this stage want to work on their terms, whether it's full-time paid work, volunteer work, consulting, board work, a new business, community involvement, or part-time endeavor. This book can help you decide if you choose to or need to work. If you do, it can help you manage this work along with the other areas of family, fitness, travel, creative activities, health challenges, pain management, financial management, and spirituality.

None of these topics by themselves is unique or earth-shattering. But, I have found that shifting your mindset, and using a combination of several of these topics, can make life more meaningful and fulfilling. At this stage, life comes first and work second, which is a change for many people from previous life stages. Ideally, life and work can be integrated for the benefit of both.

Why Another Book on Retirement and Aging?

I was looking for a book to recommend to my clients, so I started reading books written on retirement and aging. I found there are a lot of them. Please don't throw up your hands at this point and say, "What! She's writing a book on retirement and aging, too? Will these baby boomers never know when to quit?" There are many good books available related to retirement and aging, and at first I had the same reaction. Does the world really need another one?

But, I was looking for something different. I wanted a practical, comprehensive book that covers all the topics I coach my clients on regarding how to make this transition from working to retirement and the third stage of life in a holistic way. I also hope my book will disrupt many commonly held biases against aging, and promote the concept that whatever we are at this point in our lives is enough.

I also wanted a concise book that would cover the topics I consider most important, in as brief a way as possible. At this stage in life, I want to simplify things, and get to the essence of vital points directly and quickly. I find many books make concepts lengthy and complex, and I lose interest in them. It's like going to the movies now when many are two hours or more long. You lost me a half hour ago.

Many books address a specific slice of the retirement puzzle, such as those that are spiritual or internally focused, which I believe is very important at this stage. Others are focused on the body and the need to exercise and eat right, also critical to our health at this point. There are books focusing on financial preparation for retirement so you don't outlive your money. There are books helping you develop a sense of purpose and emphasizing how important relationships are to your emotional well-being. And there's a book, *This Chair Rocks: A Manifesto Against Ageism,* by Ashton Applewhite, that almost stopped me dead in my tracks. (I like the title.) Everyone needs to read this book to understand the degree to which ageism exists. We think we're aware of it, but this book goes into greater depth than other books on how pervasive it is, and how to combat it.

Yet, as specific as these books are, none of them offered a roadmap of holistic topics covering all the parts of retirement, to help people transition from working for others to the next stage of life in a simple, concise way. That's what I couldn't find, and what inspired me to write the book I wanted to read.

Some of the ideas may be unusual or provocative. People tell me I have a unique way of looking at things. You'll find there's a thread of paradox that runs through this book. If you don't agree with some of the ideas, that's great. Use whatever parts of the book apply to you. Follow your own authority.

Creating the Book

To make this book as real as possible, I interviewed many people in the third stage who are satisfied with their lives, but might do things differently if they were planning for it now. They all have good suggestions for others just starting down this road. One person retired three months ago, and another has been retired for 25 years. Some are well established financially, and others are not, and many are planning to change their lifestyle to afford to work less or not at all. Some people requested I use their entire names, and others asked me to use their first name and last initial to maintain their privacy. I'll introduce you to 13 people in the book who have all transitioned to the third stage of life in their own unique ways.

In Chapter 1, I include two interviews, one with a person recently retired and a second with someone who's been retired six years and is more settled in the retirement process. Chapters 3 and 4 also include two interviews with people who approach the topic in different ways. The other chapters include one interview at the end of each chapter. They all offer you their personal advice, and I've also included exercises to help you examine your own approach to the topics.

The first three chapters of the book focus on how to develop an identity in the third stage—one that is fulfilling and creates purpose in your life. This may or may not include work, but in most cases, work is an important part of one's identity, at least in the early years of the third stage.

The fourth chapter explores change and adversity, because the third stage of life creates more changes than earlier stages in your life, many of which may be difficult to deal with. This chapter provides a three-phase process for dealing with these changes, and how to turn adversity to your advantage.

The fifth chapter focuses on ways to care for your body and brain, and offers pain management sugges-tions, many of which I've had personal experience with. It also provides suggestions for fitness and brain health.

The sixth chapter is dedicated to spirituality and ways to develop a rich inner life to sustain you. It can help you develop an expanded consciousness and serve you well as you move into a phase of mindful aging. This is the time to become curious about all the possibilities life can offer without being attached to the outcome. At this stage of life, you learn to live from the soul and heart, not from the mind, will, or ego.

The seventh chapter focuses on personal connec-tions and the importance of interpersonal relationships with your partner, family, friends, and community. Aging is not an activity best done in isolation, but is more of a team sport, and depends on others who sup-port you and in turn benefit from your contributions. Your relationship with your partner (if you have one) is especially critical at this stage. For those who don't have a partner, family and a core group of friends will be the important connections. I find love and intimacy is very sweet and more profound at this stage of life than in previous stages, when there were many distractions from focusing on enjoying the people who matter the most to you.

The eighth chapter explores the importance of valuing your time as equally important, if not more so, than valuing financial resources. It's also a paradoxical chapter because many people think having enough money is the thing that makes the third stage of life work. I think time is the new money, as I named the chapter, and if you don't have time left, no amount of money will help. I've also discussed ways to manage both your time and your money in this chapter.

The ninth chapter explores the importance of finding creative outlets that can be nurturing and bring more learning, pleasure, and fun into your life. Curiosity and exploration can help you align with your creativity and deepest desires in ways you may not have been free enough to pursue earlier in your life.

The tenth chapter discusses how to leave a legacy and bring completion to your life in a satisfying and affirming way. It encourages you to complete things and have closure discussions with those you love while you and they are still healthy and mindful enough to do them. It also explores philanthropy for those who have the means to contribute financially to organizations and foundations.

In all the chapters, I make recommendations of other books I've read to give you more in-depth information on the topic in the chapter, and these are included in the bibliography. I've tried to be a clearing-house for trusted sources on the topics I feel are most important during your transition to the third stage of life.

In the summary, I outline the key learnings gained from the people I interviewed. They all influenced the content I developed in the chapters, and I thank them for the difference they made by giving their voices to the book, in addition to my own.

In the epilogue, I evaluate my first year of retirement life, the year I was writing this book. It's one thing to talk to others about their experiences, but another to live it yourself. Making a transition from a demanding career of 47 years without taking a break, to retiring and finding new and important ways to make a difference for myself and others can be a challenge. It's not easy to determine a new identity, but it's a change I'm excited to make, valuing the time and freedom to delve deeper into the person I'm meant to be. This book helped me start this process, and have fun at the same time. Hopefully, it can do the same for you.

Chapter 1
Time for Transformation

Are you still working and planning for your third stage of life? Or are you already in it and trying to figure out how to best use your time? The sooner you can start planning, the better, because this is a major transition that shouldn't be taken lightly. In the United States to a greater degree than in many other countries, we are identified by the work we do every day. People in other countries don't ask, "So, what do you do?" when they first meet like we do in the United States.

I was recently traveling in Italy and Mexico, and no one asked me or my husband what we did for a living. In the United States, that always seems to be the first question. Saying you're retired many times ends the conversation. People assume you have nothing new going on in your life, or nothing to add to the discussion. These are the biases we need to disrupt. Maybe the better response is to share what we are doing with our time such as, "I'm a consultant and a designer. I'm living in Mexico for part of the year and writing a book."

The people I interviewed for this book are engaged, changing their lives, trying new things, and enjoying this stage of life immensely. Not to say they don't have challenges, but they're dealing with them and moving forward. Many have used these challenges to motivate them to change their lives and communities for the better.

At this stage of life, I want to transform my identity to what my interests are now. I will still be a business coach, counselor, and consultant, but only part time because I also want to be a designer of jewelry, and work with clients to redesign and recycle jewelry they may already have into something new. These could be family pieces that are meaningful but they aren't wearing. I'm also doing jewelry trunk shows to sell the pieces I've collected over the years. As a designer, I'm interested in creating something tangible, which as a consultant I didn't do.

I want to paint and be involved in community and volunteer work, and perhaps advise new businesses or nonprofits on growth options and how to develop their culture and people. I may also want to travel and live outside the country for several months a year to experience other cultures, not just as a traveler, but as someone who lives in the community. This means my work needs to be virtual and mobile. I want to focus on my health, and reduce the pain I've had since my two surgeries. I want to spend more time with my husband, family, and friends and make new friends. I want time to focus on my inner life and develop a stronger spiritual identity. And, of course, I want to write. Sounds like a lot, but I don't have to do it all right away, or in the first year. I've got time.

When I first retired, I gave myself three months to do nothing, just to be present and see what it feels like to live without a schedule. It was very freeing, relaxing, and strange, all at the same time. We took a week-long trip outside the country to celebrate my retirement, but other than that, I used my time being instead of doing. This is a first for me because I didn't spend a lot of quiet time reflecting and doing nothing up until then. I moved into what Ron Pevny in his book, *Conscious Living, Conscious Aging*, calls the neutral zone. In this phase, we are no longer who we have been in the past, but not yet who we are to become in this next stage of life. We need to believe life has a plan for us, and to trust ourselves, because that's where the ultimate authority lies.

After this pause, I was more rested, centered, and clear about the gifts I want to offer to others in this third stage of my life. I was ready to transform how I'd been living in the past and find new adventures.

Take some time if you can as you are disengaging from your past life and getting ready to move into your new one, and see what interests and callings float to the surface for you to pay attention to. If you're still working, now is the time to start thinking about how you will substitute other activities for the meaning and accomplishment you get from your work. Whatever transformative experience you have during aging depends on your attitude toward the process.

Exercises

What things do you enjoy most in your current job (if working) or in past jobs (if not)? How will you find substitutes for those things in the third stage of your life as you retire?

_____

_____

_____

If you're working, what would you feel compelled to do when you get up each day if your current work was not in your life?

_____

_____

_____

What did you love doing as a child?

_____

_____

_____

What are your special skills that are different from those of others? What is your primary gift to offer to the world? How can you bring it forward? Don't worry about it being something big. Start small and keep going. It might turn out to be bigger than you ever expected. But, keeping it small is a good beginning because it leaves you time for other things.

_____

_____

_____

What would you do if no one was paying you to do it? If you still need to be paid, how much do you need to make, and how much of your time will that take?

_____

_____

_____

What changes would you like to bring to the world if you could?

_____

_____

_____

Where will you live and with whom or alone?

_____

_____

_____

Try to create a vivid picture of what this next stage could look like. Let it be a playful exercise, not a frustrating or intimidating one. Leave the reality for later, and now just think about options.

There are many practical considerations that need to be addressed, preferably before you leave your current job. However, there are times when you get no notice that your position is going to end and you don't have that luxury. Start planning early before you're caught by surprise by a sudden layoff or downsizing in your current job.

What about your mindset and identity? This is often the more difficult transition. *Who* do you want to be for the next 20 to 30-plus years? This is a time for intentional choices, not more of the same identity you've lived in the past, unless, of course, that is your choice. This is the time to transform your identity into the person you are at the core of your being, not the jobs you've fallen into. This can be difficult, but needs to happen to make this stage of life satisfying.

If you could start with a blank sheet knowing now what you didn't know in your 20s and 30s, what would you like to do differently? Write these things down and don't censor what comes to your mind. The more things the better, and include options that may not sound realistic.

_____

_____

_____

_____

Do you have any negative concepts about aging or retirement you need to reframe and let go of to allow you to create a new identity?

_____

_____

_____

Keep a third-stage-of-life journal to track your thoughts and feelings now that many options may become open to you that weren't before. Record things into your phone whenever you suddenly think of them. Try to broaden the scope of things to consider, and play around with exploring possibilities.

This first chapter has two interviews. They offer examples of the first steps in making this transition taken at different points in retirement.

Interview

This person I interviewed had the desire to take time off before making any decisions about her next steps. Anne G., at the age of 65, had just retired three months before we talked, and was planning to relax for the first year of her retirement to see what interests emerged. She said she had planned to wait until she was 66 to retire, but her back pain resulting from a surgery many years ago made it too difficult to continue her work as a librarian.

Then, both her parents died several months before her retirement, one a month after the other. That solidified her decision to stop working, and she is still dealing with the grief from those losses.

Because she and her husband adopted two daughters later in life, she has an 18-year-old daughter at home, so she is still "doing the mom thing," as she refers to it.

Her husband, a physician, is still working and has selected January 2019 as his retirement date. She feels fortunate she and her husband have done some financial planning and should be able to afford to maintain their lifestyle.

Anne is planning to enjoy time with cultural pursuits and the arts, and at some time she wants to become more of an art patron. She's also looking forward to traveling to visit some friends she's not seen in years to reconnect with those relationships.

Creating an identity that will make the best use of her skills, and perhaps continuing some volunteer teaching at a local public library, is important to her. Working with immigrant children in a nearby community is also an interest of hers.

Anne's recommendations for others are:

- Get in touch with your feelings about the skills you want to use in retirement and find a new community of people to relate to.

- Be open to adventure, traveling, and reconnecting with old friends.

- Give yourself time to do nothing at the beginning of your retirement if possible, so you can enjoy yourself before making any major commitments.

- Contribute to society through some type of volunteer work you find satisfying that uses your unique gifts.

- Discuss financial and other issues with your partner, especially regarding how to spend money in retirement, so you are both on the same page.

Interview

Trish R. is 73. She retired at 67 from her corporate communications consulting business in which she successfully worked for many companies while living in New

York, Chicago, and San Francisco. She loved working and would have continued, but was laid off from her last consulting position and decided to change her life. She likes to change and "shake things up" as she said, and even decided to change her name from Pat to Trish to reflect her new identity when she retired.

She put most of her retirement planning time into deciding where she wanted to live, and made sure she had the financial resources not to work, because she wasn't planning to continue her consulting. After taking trips to explore many locations, including Mexico and Santa Fe, Trish decided to relocate to Sonoma, California, in the wine country north of San Francisco. She wanted a smaller town in the country, not the suburbs, that was still close to a major city, and a place with many activities she could become involved in, as she likes doing new things all the time.

Trish said she didn't plan much what she would do with her time before retiring, choosing to let that evolve into many new areas. After joining the Sonoma Valley Newcomers organization, she soon found herself taking on leadership of a group that goes on short daytrips exploring new areas.

Trish became involved with the Sonoma Film Festival, and developed a paid position with them organizing volunteers to produce the annual event. She has always been involved with the arts and cultural activities, and still attends a film group in San Francisco. Collecting art, mainly three-dimensional works, and donating pieces to museums has been very enjoyable for her.

Trish joined the Homeowners Association Board where she lives, and she travels frequently. She recently completed a five-week trip to Africa as one of a group of 14, and plans to take one major trip a year.

Her latest venture is to become involved in politics, and she joined a new group called Women Unite to influence the 2018 elections in California.

Trish has designed an active retirement and says she wouldn't do anything differently if she was retiring today.

Trish's recommendations for others are:

- Find an organization to connect to,
  and push yourself to get out, be
  active, and meet new people.
- Take care of yourself and pace yourself by
  spending time only doing things you love.
- Try new things all the time to keep
  learning and staying interested in life.

Chapter 2
Design Thinking Creates Your Third Stage Identity

The third stage is the time to design your life in the way you ideally want to live. To identify what you'd like to focus your time on, use design thinking. Design thinking is now being championed by many people to go beyond product design, as it has traditionally been used, to solving business and community issues. It's also useful for designing your life and discovering new thinking, feelings, and purpose in ways you may not have considered previously.

Bill Burnett and Dave Evans's book, *Designing Your Life*, utilizes design thinking, and their book has made a valuable contribution to people choosing their careers. I believe design thinking can go beyond careers to apply to life in retirement. I also like Ayse Birsel's book, *Design the Life You Love*, which takes a visual approach to design thinking.

The d.school at Stanford (formerly the Hasso Plattner Institute of Design) has been a pioneer in design thinking, as has IDEO, an international design and consulting company. *Creative Confidence: Unleashing the Creative Potential Within Us All* by Tom Kelley and

David Kelley is a classic book on design thinking that provides even more detailed information.

There are now many books about design thinking, but I haven't seen one that suggests using it with people entering retirement or the third stage of life. I've used design thinking with many of my clients because it emphasizes action and experimentation, rather than simply thinking about alternatives to find your identity or the work you choose to do next. You can't make good decisions by sitting, thinking, or talking about something passively. You need to go out and try some things to decide what interests you and what doesn't.

It's called *prototyping* in the design world, and this means experimenting by doing the things you are considering. This is beyond the networking concept we're all familiar with. While you should network, and talk to people doing the work you think you'd like to do, with prototyping you find ways to begin doing it yourself on a small scale. You take a relevant class, work with a mentor or coach, volunteer in this area, get an internship, meet new people and ask them questions, reframe your thinking, write a blog, go on advisory boards, boards of directors, or set up an advisory board for yourself.

If you have the financial resources, you may want to invest in startup companies or early-stage ventures in the industry of your choice, or start your own organization or foundation. Explore ways to try on your new identity, and see what reaction you get. Notice how you feel about doing more of it. Hopefully, the reason you are interested in prototyping a specific area is because you've had experience with it at some point in your life, and have skills that could transfer, so it's realistic to create ways in which your background could fit. This new area needs to be meaningful and feasible. Once you act and immerse yourself in this new identity, you'll know if you should continue this path to explore it further, or move on to other areas to prototype.

You need to use empathy when talking to people who are giving you their perspective. Value their time and the issues they are facing, and find ways to be a resource to them when possible. Challenge your preconceived ideas, and be open to seeing things from their point of view.

I find many people at the third stage of their lives feel stuck thinking about options, are overwhelmed by a lack of action, and often fear risk. They feel they have too much to lose by taking chances this late in the game.

I believe the opposite is the better approach. Now is the perfect time to take the biggest risks of all, if they are well thought out, before you invest a great deal of time or money in them. You have no one to please but yourself, and perhaps your partner, family, or whoever will go on this journey with you. Playing it safe seems like the logical and obvious approach. But, this is a case where doing the opposite can create better solutions that are closer to who you want to become.

There's a great sailing analogy in the book, *The One Life We're Given: Finding the Wisdom that Waits in Your Heart*, by Mark Nepo. His father was a sailor who taught him the importance of getting far enough out into the sea to catch the wind. Only then out in the open will the wind show it's face and fill the sails. You can't hover too near the shore close to your old identity. Once you take a chance and steer out into the open, your soul will fill you with spirit so your smaller self has no choice but to be engaged in steering you toward what matters most to you. It takes being bold and willing to try something new to move into the larger stream of life and find your true identity.

You can make your moves in a new direction slowly to help you feel more confident. It doesn't matter if you fail. Trying something new can help you stretch your comfort level with exploring the unknown.

Keep track of all the people you connect with while prototyping so you can decide who is worth following up with, and note the feedback you get from them. There's a fine line between following up with someone and chasing them. After you've made many connections using your new identity, allow time for things to come back to you. This will also let you know if you're on the right path. Don't give up too soon. Give this new idea enough time to germinate. If opportunities start coming your way, this is an encouraging sign you may have found something that's a good fit. You can modify your thinking and change directions along the way, since that's the point of prototyping.

This testing-out process is like a minimum viable product, or MVP, in technology. What you start with you don't expect to be perfect, or the final product. You just need to get something out in the world to get feedback on so you can see if people respond in a positive way, and if you're headed in the right direction.

Apple has always done a good job of this by sending out products that aren't totally ready, but they learned what was important from the feedback of their early adopters. You don't want to wait until you think your business, product, or idea is perfect. That's too late, and you won't benefit from the thinking of many other smart people. The earlier you can put some of your work or ideas out there, the better.

I prototyped this book by sharing it with beta readers before completing the manuscript and sending it to my editor. The readers let me know when I was on the right track, and had many good ideas I added to the book that made it better. Feedback from your audience, or those you trust to be direct and honest, may feel intimidating. But, your openness to criticism or different ways to look at an issue will make you more certain of the direction you are heading in, or may cause you to change direction and save you from wasting time on an area that won't be satisfying for you.

Exercises

Identify up to three things you'd consider doing at this stage in your life that you'd like to prototype.

_____

_____

_____

How would you start to prototype the most appealing one?

_____

_____

_____

Begin with one area and research it online. Identify people you could talk to who are knowledgeable about this area. Consider taking a class or volunteering somewhere that would give you firsthand information about the area you have chosen, if you are not already familiar with it. If you have some experience already, find an organization to hire you to do some consulting in this area, or write a blog or a book about it.

If your interest fades or you decide it's not what you want to do, move to a second area to prototype and then to a third, if needed. Once you've decided you're serious about one of them, go after it in a major way and don't second-guess yourself, unless you learn new information that causes you to change your mind. Experiment. Be an adventurer!

For areas you're more familiar with, like consulting or teaching in your field of expertise, you'll know the content area, but the prototyping needed could be to set up your own business, begin marketing yourself as a consultant, or try to find work with another consulting firm or teaching at a university. If your past work experience is something you'd like to do more of, but in a different setting or as a member of a board of directors, contact search firms to explore options. Pay attention to how you feel about doing these things, and you'll get an indication of whether this could be a successful area to spend time on in the third stage of your life.

Ask everyone you know for suggestions of people doing what you think you might like to pursue. Find influencers and mentors to collaborate with in the area you are exploring, and don't worry if they decline. What do you have to lose at this stage? Be optimistic and practice feeling confident regardless of what their response is. Embrace diverse points of view, and try to find one key lesson from each person you talk to. Trust the process and have fun with it.

Interview

One of my current clients who has done a particularly good job of design thinking and prototyping is Lita Reyes. She's in her early 50s and just beginning to consider the identity she wants for the third stage of her life. She knows that the jobs she's held in the past, and the broader-based emphasis of her management consulting company she's now running, are not the exact fit for the identity she wants in her next stage. She's looking for something she feels even more passion for, and believes will make a difference in the lives of others. She wants to find her calling or a purpose to pursue for the remainder of her work life.

Together, we explored many options, and she decided the type of work she most wanted to prototype is advising philanthropists. She's already doing projects related to this, and has worked at an environmental nonprofit organization, and has held other nonprofit and corporate positions. She consulted with several ultra-high-net-worth individuals in her business, and now is drawn to focusing on this area and expanding her current clientele to create her future identity as a philanthropic advisor. She believes consulting philanthropists is the most rewarding part of her current business, and a focus on it will be most satisfying to her for the long term. It will allow Lita to give back and make a difference in the lives of many people who have resources to donate, and for the individuals and organizations who will receive support and funding.

Several things we did before she began talking with people were to modify her resume, LinkedIn profile, and her business cards. She began joining philanthropic organizations and networking extensively, always looking for meaningful ways she could add value to the people she was connecting with, as well as ways to educate herself on whether this was her true calling.

Lita was asked to join a women's philanthropic advisory board and started making connections with people who share her values and a common purpose. She also took the philanthropy training 21/64, and found it insightful on the psychology of family dynamics and intergenerational wealth transfer. Every step she has taken continues to confirm for her that she is on the right track to achieving the most fulfilling work she is meant to do for the long term.

She said she's really enjoyed doing the design thinking and prototyping because it is a creative process that satisfies her curiosity. She can try on multiple work identities to determine the best fit for her values.

Prototyping uses her strategic thinking ability, and she sees it as "realistic experimentation." She's been "relentless," as she says, in building an enduring network, and sees this process as one in which rejection or failure doesn't matter much because, unlike networking, she isn't doing this to obtain a job. She's doing it to make certain the path she is choosing is really her calling, and will be satisfying to her in the third stage of her life. Lita is also further developing a base of new contacts who are strategic partners who can be referral sources for her business, and she in turn could refer potential donors to their foundations or organizations.

She said she also believes her entrepreneurial mindset has really helped her in this process, and she's had two good role models to help develop her tenacity.

Her grandfather, her father's father, was a World War II death march on Bataan survivor in the Philippines, and lived life to the fullest. She recalls him dancing past midnight on his 80th birthday.

Her grandmother, her mother's mother, who is 96 and still living, had a military career at a time when women were not typically working outside the home, nor pursuing vocations for intellectual stimulation.

Both of Lita's grandparents inspire her. They give her confidence, and remind her that failures are only minor setbacks and nothing to fear.

Another source of reflection for her during her design thinking process was when she took a month off from her consulting business in 2007 to go to Africa and volunteer in a conservation effort to save cheetahs. She always had a strong commitment to the environment and sustainability, and this gave her an opportunity to experiment with this area of work.

Being mentored in her business by two key female philanthropists, and working with them to create multiple projects, such as an edible schoolyard for a public school district, has also influenced her.

I asked what was difficult about doing design thinking and prototyping, and she said it can at times be a slower process than she would like, and the ambiguity can be challenging. But, she has learned that ambiguity is a key part of the process, and is a "purposeful pause" to help her consolidate what she's learning and ensure she's heading down the right path toward her vision.

Lita's recommendations for others are:

- Have fun and enjoy the experience.
- Do the process with a coach or with others who have done it, so you'll have a sounding board to help you determine if the information you're receiving indicates you're on the right track.
- Start early and keep at it. Realize it takes practice and you won't be good at it right away. Don't be daunted by downtimes because they can be just as, if not more, informative in helping you consolidate what you are learning.
- Take risks and be courageous. Contact anyone you're referred to.
- Stay focused on finding the work you will love for the long haul.

Chapter 3
Paradox Thinking Expands Your Options

Paradox thinking is a different way of contemplating and resolving issues. When two words or ideas seem illogical or contradictory, they may in fact be compatible, justified, or true. There is much research available on the power of paradox thinking. Chinese sages call it the law of reverse effort. Paradox thinking goes against the flow of generally accepted ways of viewing issues. It's a both/and approach that allows you to hold two seemingly opposing ideas in your mind at the same time. As Lao Tzu said, "All behavior consists of opposites . . . learn to see things backwards, inside out, and upside down."

I've always liked paradoxes, and I'm a believer in seeing things in opposite ways. Remember we are trying to disrupt conventional ways of thinking about aging and retirement, so exploring opposite ways of thinking can push you toward new ideas.

Paradox thinking can also be very important at this stage of your life because you will face obstacles, and can benefit from seeing them as ways to look creatively at other options. You can change your perspective to make these obstacles the very things that strengthen your resolve to try a different approach. When I was at my former company, I founded the Leadership Development and Executive Coaching practice, and we created a leadership model based on paradox called Core, Edge, and Agility. In a research study we conducted, we interviewed over 100 individuals at different companies and organizations. Our results showed that the best leaders were those who can shift their focus and energy quickly from dealing with things that are known to them (core) to dealing with something totally unknown to them (edge). This shifting of energy and focus, especially if it happens many times during a day, demands personal agility. Our results showed that using these opposite behaviors defined as core and edge create energy, and develop the strongest, most creative leaders and teams, as defined by the people who work with them.

I find the same type of paradox thinking can expand your scope of options at this stage by considering opposites to help you feel you've left no stone unturned, no passion unexplored.

This may make you feel you are in a place of ambiguity and don't know which direction to take. This is a good thing, because being in a state of ambiguity requires wisdom to not rush to a quick solution. Take time to challenge yourself to consider new options. If you're not feeling a bit uncomfortable or unsure about the new things you're considering, you're probably not stretching yourself enough.

Paradox thinking sounds simple, but may be hard to get your mind to accept. We're used to thinking as being a rational exercise to create practical solutions to issues. However, paradox thinking can be very freeing and can stimulate creativity to exercise your thought muscles and consider both ends of the spectrum and everything in between.

William Sadler and James Krefft in their book, *Changing Course: Navigating Life After 50*, emphasize the importance of building a new identity based on paradox, and how it can limit your options to be focused on an either/or approach. Paradox thinking as a concept may be easy to grasp, but it requires regular practice to come naturally as a tool for creativity. Start by having an open, curious, and skeptical mind. Feel comfortable learning to hold a level of tension when exploring opposites, and let go of looking for the right answer of what to do now. Lean into the wisdom that there is no one right answer, but many. Competing ideas can lead to the most innovative solutions. This is not an approach of overanalyzing options with the hope that one will become the obvious winner. Instead it gives you the freedom to explore opposite ends of an idea, thinking that both things could be possible, then combining the varied results to create a stronger outcome than either idea by itself could have borne.

The Power of Paradox is a comprehensive book written by Deborah Schroeder-Saulnier, and in it she uses many examples of paradoxes we can integrate into our lives.

Several paradoxes I use with my clients are:

- Privacy and accessibility
- Material success and meaningful life
- Leadership and followership
- Change and stability
- Control and freedom
- External focus and internal needs
- Intuitive and analytical
- Formal and informal
- Separate and intimate
- Task and people
- Consensual and persuasive
- Candor and diplomacy
- Be and do
- Accept and challenge
- Care deeply and remain objective

How many of these opposites do you want in your life now? Brainstorm additional paradoxes that are important to you. When you make use of paradox thinking, you are better able to consider and manage what can be conflicting objectives. You won't have unlimited time to do everything you want, and still have quiet time to be mindful of all the valuable changes taking place for you internally at this stage in your life. You want to feel free to choose any combination of activities that feels right to you, though these may seem erratic or opposite to others. Your goal is to develop the wisdom to take a more holistic and expansive point of view as you age, to create a life that works best for you, without being concerned about outward appearances. At this stage of life, it's important to integrate your internal and external worlds and hold the tension this paradox creates, which will allow you to see more options as possibilities.

An example of a paradox I use frequently with my clients is "holding on and letting go." This means once you've explored several possibilities in detail by using design thinking and prototyping, and have tried different ways to make each option work, it's time to select one and go for it in a bigger way.

Holding on means staying committed to the concept until you see whether it will work. Too many options circulating in your mind will cause confusion and undermine your focus on which option to pursue. This doesn't mean you can't do several things at once, but you want to feel fully committed and focused on each one while you're pursuing them. You can add others once you've reached a conclusion about the first direction you're prototyping.

"Holding on and letting go" can also refer to the filtering process you need to go through at this stage of your life. You need to determine which relationships and things in your life bring satisfaction, and which you should let go. It could be physical things in your home that are no longer important and nurturing to have around, or relationships that drain your energy. Your goal is to spend time only doing the things that give you a sense of purpose and fulfillment. You're trying to create space for new areas of focus.

Learning to say "no" creates time for all the things you want to say "yes" to. This is not easy to do because we're all used to spending time on what others ask or tell us to do. Whether it's an employer, partner, or friend, we tend to agree to do things that others suggest without considering whether it's how we want to spend our time.

Exercises

Identify a paradox or several that you've been struggling with, or develop a set of seemingly opposite things that both attract you, and describe a way you might be able to do both. You can also use the list on the previous page. Then identify the ones you want to begin with by ranking the most important paradoxes or listings that seem 3 times or 5 times more important than the others. Then select the ones you would like to include in your life.

_____

_____

_____

What changes would be required for you to accept doing things that may seem different or opposite to the way you have thought in the past?

_____

_____

_____

Interview

Richard R. is now 77 and has been an attorney his entire career, mainly in private practice. He has now been retired from law for one year, but his planning process has been a bit of a paradox because he decided to plan for his retirement by *not* planning and avoided making any decisions about it. As a result, he never really decided to retire. Through most of his life, he has been resistant to planning. The best-laid plans of mice and men. . . . He says planning can create expectations, which might lead to disappointment if the plan is not achieved. His process was to just let it evolve and, as he says, eventually the phone stopped ringing with work, so he said, "I guess that means I'm retired," and he's very happy about it.

Richard says he's found satisfaction in retirement by having "relatively low expectations" and enjoying the little things. He discovered in retirement that he has become more solitary and contemplative. Because his past work involved the practical problems of others, he wishes to explore a more solitary life. He listens to music (mostly classical), practices his golf swing, reads (political, philosophy, and science). He loves to explore the natural world by taking walks. He also enjoys his family and friends. He likes to take road trips, primarily in California to be close to the beauty of nature. He's not fond of long-distance air travel, because of its effect on the climate.

He says he's hoping things pretty much stay the same as they are currently. He describes himself as a "lucky pessimist," an interesting paradox, who imagines the worst but thinks it won't happen to him because he's been fortunate. He's frugal and has enough money to live simply and maintain his current lifestyle.

His wife is younger and still working, but is getting ready to retire soon, and his children are on their own and doing well. He doesn't have any driving desire to leave a specific legacy, as he says, and has been healthy up until now, and is hoping to be brave enough to endure pain, both emotional and physical, which may come with aging.

His parents provided him good role models. Both parents lived simply and happily into their 90s.

Richard's suggestions for others are:

- Have realistic expectations for retirement and be happy doing the simple things.
- Become a "lucky pessimist," as he says, and don't do things you don't want to do.
- Don't plan too much, focus on the present, and be grateful to live your life each day.

He realizes this may be the opposite of what many people think you should do to prepare for retirement, but it's working well for him, and he plans to maintain lucky pessimism so he can keep doing it. I like using Richard's interview since it's the opposite of the preparation I would normally suggest in this book, but it works for him, and shows that there are many right ways to get to the goal of identifying a satisfying third stage of life.

Interview

Steve S. has an MBA in Finance, and worked his way up to being Global Head of Risk Management at a large financial institution where he'd worked for 31 years and had 250 people reporting to him. He was 56 years old when he retired, and the demands of his job—often requiring 14 to 16 hour days and constant travel—were becoming unsatisfactory. He found he was having a hard time getting out of bed in the morning, and decided he didn't want to keep up that pace anymore.

Steve was young at 56 when he decided it was time to retire from his position. When he told his manager, several people suggested other positions or perhaps some part-time work to keep him with the company. While he appreciated their offers, he knew it was time for a change. It took him two years to finish up projects, and find and train his replacement before he could finally make the move, and he was so busy he hardly had time to think about what came next.

It felt strange to not have a job because he never had that experience, and he describes it as a double-edged sword, both scary and liberating. He took a risk many people might not have been willing to take after maneuvering his way into a very senior level role. He did the opposite of what many expected, and left his job at age 58 without knowing what he would do next. But, he knew it was the right thing, and he wanted to leave while he was still at the top of his game.

Steve also didn't think of himself as retiring in the traditional sense of the word because he knew he wasn't going to just relax and play golf all day. He planned to have the same kind of active retirement the other people I've interviewed have. As he says, "It's not your father's retirement anymore." He knew he would find a new identity and a way to make an impact, and he found it in teaching. It's now been two years since he left the corporate world, and he's teaching at a local college as an adjunct professor in microeconomics and really enjoying it. It's much more time consuming than he anticipated, requiring 7 to 10 hours to prepare for a one-and-a-half-hour class, so he feels like he's still working hard. But, he enjoys motivating students and finding ways to present information in a relevant way that focuses on the business impact, not just the traditional economic principles. Steve doesn't have a PhD in economics, but real-world experience, which can be to his advantage. He wants to leverage his background to help develop the next level of business managers.

He's not sure what comes next, but the idea of "taking it on the road," as he says, is appealing to him. He always lived in New York or New Jersey, and he'd like to live some place new for a semester or two. He'd consider Texas, Oklahoma, or somewhere in the Midwest as options to experience a different, more down-to-earth lifestyle.

Steve's children are grown, and his youngest is a sophomore in college. His wife quit working after their second child was born, and she's not working now. He'd need to get her buy-in before planning any move, but thinks she might be open to it. He'd also consider going back to school himself at the age of 60 to take a class in something that interested him.

Steve says if he could do it over again, he would have planned more for the transition and managed it better. He would have liked to have explored his options more in advance, but it took him so long to unwind from his job that there wasn't time.

Steve's suggestions for others are:

- Don't be afraid to leave a job. He knows others who would like to, but the fear factor gets in the way. Some people literally die at their desks or soon after retiring. We define ourselves so much by work that it can feel scary to stop. But, he has learned you can re-define yourself, so encourages others to not resist making a move.

- Make it happen on your terms.
  Embrace the change.

- Don't hang on too long. He says, "You don't want to be like Willie Mays falling in the outfield when you're too old to play."

Chapter 4

Change and Adversity
Can Be an Advantage

You will likely experience more change and adversity at this period in your life than during previous years. Your body may be weakening, you may have endured illnesses and injuries, and you may not be able to run or play some of your favorite sports. You're soon to experience the losses of friends and loved ones, if you haven't already. You may have been laid off your job. It's easy to see why many people in their 60s through 90s feel the deck is stacked against them.

Because of this, we need to get creative and find replacements for our losses. It won't ever be the same as it was, there's no denying that. But, we need to find a way to stop wishing things were different, or they won't ever be.

You're going to be unhappy when these things occur, and I suggest you try using a simple process that includes these three things:

- Acknowledge the loss or change you're experiencing. Don't diminish it or act like it isn't happening. The door is closing on that part of your life. Don't stick your foot in the way and hope to keep it open. It won't work, and you'll continue to feel miserable. Expect to go through denial and anger at this stage.

- Give yourself sufficient time to grieve the change or loss thoroughly for however long it takes before you can let go. This will be a different amount of time for each person depending on the degree of change and type of loss. Be thankful for the opportunity you had to do the things in your past, or the years you had that person in your life. Realize that you won't "get over it," as some people tell you, but in time you will develop the internal fortitude to live with it, and hopefully use this adversity as material for your personal growth.

- Search for a new door to open. It's there somewhere, but it won't open on its own. You need to begin actively looking for it, and turn a few doorknobs. Don't give up. You will always have the experiences of your past, or the person you loved with you. But, try to make lemonade, because I'm sure at the stage in your life you feel like you have plenty of lemons. Find the new gift you might have missed offering to the world if the change or loss hadn't occurred. Collaborate with others to create a change that's important to you. Be patient with yourself, stay in the present, and give yourself positive feedback for how well you're doing. Expect to slip backwards certain days, but don't be concerned if you can get up the next day and move forward.

As Ryan Holiday discusses in his book, *The Obstacle Is the Way*, it's hard to imagine it's possible, but you can use a setback or adversity to your advantage. Difficulties are material for you to work with, to create something new.

This isn't new thinking. Roman emperors and philosophers like Marcus Aurelius and Seneca, and people like Steve Jobs and Amelia Earhart, all figured out how to do this before any of us did. So much relies on our perception, creativity, and will, and these are things we can change, if we choose to.

Exercises

Have you experienced some loss or adversity in your life you would like to not only overcome, but learn to use to your advantage? If so, describe it.

_____

_____

_____

Have you thoroughly grieved your loss?

_____

_____

_____

Can you think of something you can experiment with or someone you could contact who could help you find a new door to open? This could be a therapist, a friend, something you read, or some new work you'd like to try.

_____

_____

_____

Would you choose to continue doing some parts of your current or past jobs? Would you consider becoming an entrepreneur? If so, what type of work would you open a business in?

_____

_____

_____

What parts of these jobs appeal to you, and how much time would you spend doing them? Are there things you could delegate to make this more possible?

_____

_____

_____

Other than a job, what else could you imagine may fill the gap . . . something you might have never thought to try if this negative experience hadn't happened?

_____

_____

_____

Interview

A person who is an inspiration for me in how to overcome chronic pain and turn it to your advantage is Dr. P. She is a psychiatrist who began suffering from chronic pain 25 years ago when she was 38. She was in a faculty position at a major university in her dream job, and had a thriving private practice. She was happily married, had a two-year-old son, she and her husband bought their first house, and life was going well.

Suddenly, her body began experiencing widespread pain, insomnia, numbness, tingling, vertigo, irritable bowel syndrome, fatigue, and balance problems. She was unable to sleep even using medication.

She knew many good doctors in the area, and began searching for the cause of her pain. She and her husband were extremely frightened, and they consulted with 14 well-meaning physicians. After many diagnostic tests and multiple diagnoses including Multiple Sclerosis, she was put on five strong daily medications.

The medications allowed her to work for seven more years until her body crashed at age 45, and she was bedridden. It was a struggle to walk 10 feet from her bedroom to the bathroom without falling into both walls.

She was outraged, had feelings of grief and resistance, and kept wanting to fix her body, change it, or at least know what was causing this.

She gradually learned she had to let go, stop searching for answers, and start to love her body just as it was—sick and broken. She began to tune-in to her body, something she was never taught in medical school. She shifted her attitude from fixing her body to respecting that it was doing the best it could. She sent it love and approval, and began making minor changes, and gradually weaned herself off the medications and experienced withdrawal.

Dr. P. noticed the key to slow, gradual improvement was to "lighten the load" on her body and mind. Reducing stressful thinking quieted her mind to allow it to not take energy from her body. She began reading books, singing a cappella, going outside in nature and laying on a yoga mat, which all seemed to help. Gradually, she could eventually walk and hike again.

Given the financial challenges of not being able to work, she started a women's group on the topic of money. Her first action was to refinance the mortgage on their house, saving a considerable amount. She also started a women's group on health issues.

She began seeing a trainer, changed to a plant-based diet, received weekly bodywork, practiced daily brain retraining and daily journal work. She says she learned to let go of worry about others, and to trust they will find their own path.

After many "flare-ups," as she calls them, she went back to her notes to see what she had done in the past that worked. She paid attention to details and triggers such as allergic reactions, changes in the seasons or temperature. Anything that would bring on a new episode of pain were important factors to consider.

Dr. P. is now 63, her pain is under control, and she says she views the past 25 years as a blessing. It enabled her to cultivate her marriage and spend time with her husband and son, and caused her to simplify her life and learn to live within her limitations. We have a stressful culture, and anything we can do to lighten the load on our bodies will help them to function better.

She learned to "trust life," as she says, and have compassion. Fear comes from not trusting, and she advises us to believe in our bodies and the messages they give us, and to find support in others. Turn inward to develop a healthy inner-directed life, ask for wisdom, and do whatever you can to increase the energy in your body.

Friends noticed the major changes in her, and began asking if she could help others they knew were struggling. A consulting practice gradually began in her home, which she now manages at a sustainable pace. She has helped me and many others, and we all feel grateful she's found her true calling.

The suggestions Dr. P. would give to others are:

- Bodies are temporary; however, we are infinite beings. Regardless of what happens to the body, we can thrive internally in our souls.
- Cultivate joy and freedom. Respect your body, care for it, and answers will find you.
- Follow your intuition and your own authority. Be your own best advocate.
- Be who you are and trust the Power that knows the way.

Work Only on Your Own Terms

One of the ways you can choose to deal with adversity is to do some work in this period of life to help you overcome whatever loss you have experienced. If this is the case for you, make sure you do it on your terms, if possible. As I said earlier, retirement doesn't mean you won't choose to work. An AARP/National Council on Aging report showed that 80 percent of Americans will be retired by the time they are 70, but *60 percent* of these retirees will move into new lines of work. And 1 in 10 people in their 80s will still be working.

Many people I've interviewed enjoy the work they've done in the past, and don't want to leave it altogether. That's good if you're the one who gets to decide how and when you're working, which parts of the job you'll keep doing, and what you'll let go of. This depends on your economic situation, and many people at this stage of life don't have the financial resources to leave their past work behind, or to work only on their own terms.

However, there are ways to reduce the stress a nonstop focus on work can cause. A certain level of stress is motivating and energizing. Too much of it is debilitating, very difficult on your body, and can make you sick. The root cause of many illnesses can be traced back to high levels of stress or cortisol in your system.

I help many people start their own businesses at this point in their lives, because there are fewer good jobs available once you're past 60. These businesses could be part-time, consulting, writing, and may involve delegating the pieces of the job that are most stressful, if that's an option for you. This may be more possible for those with a professional career or practice, such as a doctor, therapist, accountant, counselor, teacher, writer, or someone who can afford to hire others to do the parts of the work they don't like.

Most work can be done virtually, at least part of the time, and this can bring you more flexibility. Research indicates that having the freedom to set your own schedule has been shown to be more valuable to many people than receiving a raise. Time and flexibility can be more important than money at this stage of your life, if you have your basic needs covered.

Interview

One of the best examples I've seen of someone who is overcoming health challenges while continuing to do the work he's enjoyed all his life, but now totally on his terms, is Dr. Dave S. in San Francisco. He's best known as the founder of the Haight Ashbury Free Clinic in 1967, and he hasn't slowed down much since then. At the age of 78, he has his own clinical practice and is the author of 26 books, a frequent lecturer, and a sponsor of the annual Symposium and San Francisco Addiction Summit.

He's a champion of mission-driven health-care, and is preserving the legacy he helped create by advocating for healthcare as a right, not a privilege. He's very hands-on in the philanthropic work he does, such as the scholarship fund he established in Bakersfield, California, where his mother was a nurse, and he attends the ceremony every year to present a $5,000 scholarship to a high school student to pursue a career in healthcare.

He said he's defined the range of activity he wants to work within at this stage in his life by delegating administrative and fundraising activities he used to be involved with, and has stopped doing any lengthy travel based on health limitations. At this point he says he "only goes where he wants to go." He lives within two blocks of his office, and has established a strong support system to help him continue to make contributions to public service, which he strongly believes in. He's also committed to learning new things, and said he and his wife recently joined a book club, since they're both avid readers.

At this stage of life, he says he's "not a hot commodity, but a historical figure." He's contributed in a major way to the medical field, and his approach to treatment of addiction as a disease instead of a moral deficiency or criminal activity has advanced the concept of nonjudgmental healthcare.

Dr. Dave's created a purposeful and fulfilling third stage of life for himself and the many people he touches every day, and he does it on his terms while overcoming illnesses or difficult things that have occurred in his life. I'd say that makes him a very hot commodity we can all learn from.

Dr. Dave's suggestions for others are:

- Continue to do work you believe in to contribute to public service.
- Pace yourself and only do things you have the energy for and enjoy.
- Don't allow illnesses or health challenges to keep you from doing what you want.
- Acknowledge your limitations and don't do things exceeding them.
- Take a hands-on approach and give back to the community.

These examples both deal with health issues as a source of adversity. But, I have also known many clients who have experienced other areas of adversity to over-come. I know several people who thought they really wanted to get a new job when they were laid off their past jobs. After long and difficult job searches that depressed them, they ended up letting go of this option.

Instead, they started businesses that became very satisfying to them, and they never would have con-sidered entrepreneurship if they had found new posi-tions working for other organizations. Now they are very pleased they never got the jobs they thought they wanted.

I've also heard from people whose adult children returned home after college and grad school because they couldn't afford to live on their own. At first this really upset the parents because they were looking forward to time and freedom as a couple at this stage of their lives. However, once they lived through the transition, it brought them closer as a family and they were happy to have had the time to live together again at this stage of their lives. Thankfully, it didn't last forever, or it might not have felt like an advantage!

Chapter 5
Body, Brain, and Pain

Pain Management

As you're identifying how you want to spend this time in your life, you may experience pain or an illness you didn't have before you were in the third stage of life. Unfortunately, for many of us it will be chronic pain, which is very difficult to identify the cause of, and harder still to eliminate. Most of us didn't consider pain management to be an important issue earlier in our lives, because we probably didn't experience the same type of pain we may have now in our 60s or 70s.

I had a surgery in my 40s, and it was difficult and painful, but I recovered from it quickly. I had always felt very healthy and never gave much thought to pain.

That is until I was 62 and one day while walking through the Irvine, California, airport pulling my luggage, I got a sharp, stabbing pain in my back that almost made me fall to the ground. I never had any back problems, so I was shocked to have this pain that wouldn't go away.

After spending two years going to six different back specialists, getting six MRIs, seeing acupuncturists, chiropractors, physical therapists, neurologists, pain management specialists, attending yoga classes, and receiving injections, nothing helped. Then I was referred to an endocrinologist who suggested an MRI of my stomach, which showed I had a large "flank incision hernia" in my back, an inch from my spine, with an opening that was 6x6 inches in size! I had never heard of such a thing, and it's a rare occurrence to have the previous incision from a surgery 25 years ago to open, and for my large intestine to push through the incision taking my kidney with it, creating a chronic pain that no medication helped.

I've learned a lot about chronic pain since I still have it even after two hernia surgeries finally repaired the hernia, but didn't totally relieve the pain. Cutting through tissues, nerves, and moving organs creates new pain. After five years, I'm learning to manage the pain and it's greatly improved, but I haven't been able to make it go away totally. Strong pain medications, such as opioids, make me dizzy and nauseous, which makes it impossible to work. Over-the-counter medications like Ibuprofen and Tylenol don't reduce the pain.

Keeping a positive frame of mind, and being tenacious about finding ways to realign my body and strengthen my core have reduced the pain somewhat, as well as reading books about how others have dealt with chronic pain and talking with people who face this daily. Meditation and mindfulness are topics I'll address in a later chapter, and they have also helped reduce the pain. Music, such as the CDs you can find on centerpointe.com, can change your brainwaves to release pain. You can listen to these at night to help you sleep or during the day to increase your relaxation.

There is also now a spinal cord high-frequency stimulation implant which is having good results in treating back and leg pain.

If you are experiencing pain, look for the best doctors and pain specialists in your community because someone is going to be able to help you. The key is to not give up, and you will eventually find someone you trust. I found many good doctors who tried various approaches, and I worked with two excellent doctors who repaired my hernia. But, in terms of pain management, working with bodywork professionals regularly helped me more than traditional doctors, even those who are pain management specialists.

Developing a new mindset that allows me to think of pain as a sensation has helped. I've learned not to take the pain personally, and how important it is to be a nurturing caretaker of my body, rather than feeling upset that it continues to hurt. This is easier said than done when you feel like your body is torturing you with continuous pain, and you feel exhausted and resentful about it.

I've learned I need to relax into the pain as much as possible to increase my tolerance of it, and allow my body to heal. This isn't easy to do, and I've never experienced anything as challenging as living with chronic pain while still maintaining an optimistic view about the future.

However, pain can also be a tool to give you the courage to change your life. Many people tolerate jobs or living situations that cause them to feel stress to the degree that their bodies create pain, and the only way to eliminate it is to change the situation. In these scenarios, pain is a gift.

Once I retired, I made my health a top priority and used some of my newly found time to focus on body-work, exercise, hydration, and eating right. In addition to removing the stress that a high-pressure job can create, these practices all contributed to reducing my pain.

I learned it's important to unwind your central nervous system for pain to subside. Changing your central nervous system from the sympathetic, fight-or-flight system, to the parasympathetic, a more relaxed and resting state, can reduce the level of your pain. Physical therapists and osteopaths can give you exercises to help with this transition, and there are anxiolytic medications that can accelerate this shift, which a doctor who is a pain management specialist or psychiatrist may decide to prescribe for you.

Fortunately, not everyone who experiences aging will experience pain. If you do, the following are ways that I and others I have interviewed have learned to live with chronic pain and still function well in our daily lives, making the most of the third stage of life.

Exercise and Self-Care

Everyone knows how important exercise is, and when we were younger many of us worked out regularly, making fitness and exercise an integrated part of our life. It is even more critical to do this in the third stage of life. Unfortunately, many people find it harder to do at this point. You may be in pain from an injury or surgery, or lack the stamina you had earlier in your life. But, self-care for your body and brain should be a key part of the daily routine you build into this third stage of life.

Walking every day as much as possible helps retain your balance and aerobic health, and lifting light weights maintains muscle mass. Riding a bike or taking spinning classes helps improve your balance, strengthens your muscles, and provides aerobics and stamina.

Working with a physical therapist or trainer can be helpful to stay focused on your workout. I've worked with a physical therapist who is a pain management specialist. She's given me a series of exercises I do at home in between phone calls and client sessions. She helped me learn the value of stretching, floor exercises, yoga, and using exercise videos or DVDs. Another home workout is a rebounder, which is a small trampoline, to strengthen your legs and improve the circulation of your lymph system. Having exercise equipment at home is helpful when the weather is poor, which gives many of us an excuse to avoid the gym or going out for a hike.

PBS has programs such as *Essentrics* by Miranda Esmonde-White that air daily to help us focus on strengthening muscle cells, which she believes is the key to healthy longevity. These programs are 30 minutes long and can make a huge difference in muscle tone, balance, and flexibility. She's also written a book, *Aging Backwards*.

Floor exercises like those I learned in Pilates and yoga have made it easy to take a break in my home office and do these exercises for 15 minutes.

We've all heard exercises that build a strong core are key to a strong back. Sitting for long periods of time is one of the worst things to do for our bodies' health. Even though I use a standing desk, I can't stand constantly either, so laying down on the floor or bed and "de-weighting," as my physical therapist calls it, is a help to my back. This just means lying down to relax and doing nothing else during this time. It can be for 5 or 10 minutes, but will still make a big difference in your body's health.

"Sitting is the new smoking," a phrase coined by Dr. James Levine at the Mayo Clinic, is worth considering. Being sedentary or sitting or standing for many hours is not healthy and can result in pain. Movement is the key to long-term health and cell regeneration. This doesn't mean we can make up for a day of little movement by going to the gym or taking a walk. While those are important things to do, I've learned you need to get up and move every half hour, whether it's walking to the next room or up and down stairs or walking around the office while on a conference call. The key is to get your circulation moving on a regular basis. However, we need to be moving in the right way with our bodies aligned correctly.

Pete Egoscue's book, *Pain Free*, explores the ways our bodies may not be aligned correctly, and this may cause pain. He also outlines many exercises to realign the body, which my husband and I both do.

Taking our well-being seriously, and integrating it into our culture and workplaces would address this vital issue even before moving into the third stage of life. However, many workplaces provide constant stress and ask for more continuous activity than our bodies can tolerate for long periods without downtime. We need to regularly disengage so our bodies can destress. Unfortunately, it's become a badge of honor at many workplaces to overextend, and this accelerates the aging process at any time in your life. When you put your nervous system into overdrive, stress hormones are excreted that deprive your cells of the ability to restore themselves. Too much stress ages bodies.

Myofascial Release

The other helpful treatment for me in eliminating pain after my surgeries is myofascial release, which is a very focused deep massage used to reduce congestion in the tissues of the body. This type of bodywork can reduce scar tissue or acid deposits built up after an accident, surgery, or a prolonged period of stress. After nerves and tissues have been cut during surgery and muscles moved, white blood cells flood the area and can create an acidic buildup, putting pressure on the nerves and muscles and creating pain. This is something most doctors don't inform you about after surgery or an accident. Many are not even aware of it.

Fascia, which is like a plastic wrap layer of tissue under the skin and around all organs of the body, can become rigid and cause restrictions in our bodies. This can cause pain, decreased mobility, instability, and falls.

It can be painful to have this type of myofascial or deep tissue massage done, but it's the only way the built-up acid deposits or scar tissues can be released from the body. It's difficult to find a bodyworker who is good at doing this, and is willing to focus primarily on the areas of the body where the deposits have collected. Once you find someone, it's beneficial to see the bodyworker regularly, even once or twice a week, to have these deposits removed. Once they're removed, the body can heal itself, which it's very good at doing, if there are no blockages.

Hydration is also very important, especially after the deposits are released into your blood system. You want to flush these released deposits out of your body, and drinking water with electrolytes is helpful with this.

Healing, or anti-aging, starts at the cellular level, and hydration keeps cells from shriveling. Dehydration results in weakness, foggy thinking, and muscle fatigue, and accelerates aging and poor health. While drinking more water is critical, it won't resolve the problem of acidic blockage by itself because the cells are often not capable of absorbing it until the blockage is removed.

You can also do some of this bodywork yourself using the treatment that Sue Hitzmann teaches in her book, *The Melt Method*, using foam rollers and small balls to stimulate the connective tissues and eliminate inflammation. Partners can also work on each other using massage tools or your hands to break up deep deposits.

It's easy to blame stiffness or pain on aging because we've had more time to accumulate chronic dehydration and a buildup of inflammation and acidity. It's an ongoing process to keep the deposits from returning, but bodywork, combined with hydration, monitoring pH levels, and modifying eating habits, can help keep it from returning.

Alkaline vs. Acidic

Every day our bodies create acid deposits. To keep the body from becoming acidic and to keep acid deposits from forming, it's helpful in eliminating pain if we can create an alkaline, instead of an acidic, environment in our bodies. This means a reading of between 7 and 8 on a pH test. If you remember from school chemistry, 7 is considered neutral and the numbers below it acidic, while 8 and above is alkaline. Alkaline is the goal for healing our bodies and keeping them at maximum health. Between 7.2 and 8.4 is said to be an ideal range. You can test your first morning urine pH (not saliva) by buying strips at Amazon or the health food store.

For those who have an acidic body, myofascial release can restore health and energy and return your body to a more alkaline environment. This needs to be accompanied by eating the right foods to maintain that alkalinity. Low carbohydrate vegetables, avocados, greens, sprouts, pomegranates, lemons, and limes are all high alkalizing foods.

Taking "tri-salts," which is a supplement containing 450 mg of calcium, 250 mg of magnesium, and 99 mg of potassium, can help keep your pH at a good level. It only requires 1/2 to 1 teaspoon, and can be purchased on Amazon or at any health food store.

Drops can be added to water to make it more alkaline. I use a brand called Alka Vision Plasma pH, or you can buy water that already has high pH and electrolytes in it.

Other supplements such as amino acids, magnesium, or products to increase protein levels if they are low can help reduce pain. But, talk with your doctor or healthcare professional before you experiment with these.

Acidity in our bodies causes loss of energy, inflammation, and hardening of soft tissues, which can contribute to diseases. Maintaining healthy, alkaline blood and tissues creates a healthy body. We assume many illnesses are the result of aging, when they can be caused by an acidic condition in our bodies, which can be eliminated.

Brain Health

I won't attempt to tell you how many foods and supplements impact the health of our brains, since it would take an entire book, and there are many books now available on brain health. Several I've found helpful are by neurologist Dr. David Perlmutter. His latest book, *Brain Maker*, was published in 2015, and his earlier book, *Grain Brain,* was published in 2013. He makes a very convincing case for the direct connection between our gut and our brain, meaning what we eat directly results in brain health or illnesses such as Alzheimer's, cognitive impairment, depression, arthritis, diabetes, and migraines. He proposes eliminating grains from your eating plan for this reason.

Other good books on this topic include *The Brain Warrior's Way* by Dr. Daniel and Tana Amen and *The Brain Fog Fix* by Dr. Mike Dow. For those entering the third stage of life, it's critical to be aware of the impact that carbohydrates, grains, and sugar has on the aging process. A gluten (or grain) free, high-fat, low-carb diet can make these remaining years much more enjoyable and energetic. Few of us choose to eliminate these items altogether, but having a goal of achieving an 80/20 ratio (80% vegetables, protein and some fruit, and 20% of other foods such as carbohydrates) can add healthy years to our lives.

Sugar is a toxic element, and it can increase pain. As much as you can, avoid it by using Stevia, or Lakanto Monkfruit, both natural, organic sweeteners that are gluten free and low glycemic. Your body will benefit if you can reduce cravings for sweet things and eat them only as exceptions, rather than a regular part of your eating plan. The less you eat them, the less you'll crave them. Dark chocolate (80% or higher) may be the exception to this, and many books and doctors say there are benefits to eating one piece a day.

Books such as *Whole 30* by Melissa and Dallas Hartwig can provide an eating plan to reset your body to promote a healthy immune function and minimize inflammation. There are many eating plans promising major changes, and it's hard to know which ones to believe or follow. Talk to your doctor or healthcare professional and do some research to find one that works for you.

Caloric restriction, meaning simply reducing the amount we eat, has also been shown to create dramatic improvements in memory and cognitive functions. Periodic, short fasting periods of 24 to 48 hours can also reset your digestion, although fasting can be controversial. Changing eating habits is difficult, but the results are impressive, and I'd rather have less grain and sugar now and more brain power in my later years.

There are many other health-related topics worth discussing such as prebiotics, probiotics, healthy fats, and maintaining a ration of 2 to 1 of omega 3 to omega 6 by eating fish low in mercury. You can find many other books that cover these in more detail than I can here, but I believe it is critical to pay attention to these health-related issues as we age. There's no magic pill or elixir, but a combination of several of these approaches can make a difference in the way you feel, and in the quality of your health in the third stage of life. As a doctor recently said to me, it's important to modify your eating habits every 10 years. However, many people eat the same way in their 70s as they did in their 30s. Our bodies can't continue this and stay healthy.

The other aspect of maintaining a healthy mind is to manage your thoughts. Our thoughts can make us sick, or at least very stressed out. Byron Katie's books are good resources for managing your thought process by asking four simple questions. *Loving What Is,* her first book, and her most recent book, *A Mind at Home with Itself: How Asking Four Questions Can Free Your Mind, Open Your Heart, and Turn Your World Around,* are both useful in changing the way we think and communicate with ourselves. Her approach is that pain in life may not be optional, but suffering is based on what we say to ourselves. When we become open to questioning our stressful thoughts and whether they are truthful, they will release us and allow us to shift our thinking of the world and our perception of ourselves.

Exercises

What new things could you try to improve your fitness, reduce pain, or strengthen your brain's health?

_____

_____

_____

Are there things that have worked for you in the past that you could share with others?

_____

_____

_____

What negative thoughts do you have that bring you unhappiness or pain? How could you turn these thoughts around to consider the opposite of what you've been telling yourself?

_____

_____

_____

Interview

Terrie Carpenter is a physical therapist and pain management specialist, and she is extremely knowledgeable about the connections between the body, the brain, and pain. Terrie grew up in a small town in the Central Coast of California, and after high school attended SF State University. Her curious mind led her to explore several majors before deciding on Physical Therapy, and fortunately it turned out that SF State was the only school in the United States at that time with a Pre-Physical Therapy major.

She's encountered three important mentors in her life, and after hearing one of them, Captain Sue Osbourne, a recruiter for the Army Medical Specialist Corps, speak to her professional organization, she went on to get a direct commission in the Army to complete her physical therapy training. This was in 1968, and not a popular thing to do at the time because of the Vietnam War. Terrie trained for an additional 13 months in Texas and learned to become a "thinking therapist" as she worked on soldiers returning from the war in acute care facilities, including the burn unit. She learned to be innovative and always think outside the box when developing treatment plans for her very complex patients.

After leaving the Army and returning to San Francisco, she spent several years working at a major medical center where she was encouraged to continue her innovative approach to patient care.

In 2001, she began a five-year alliance with physicians and psychologists treating chronic pain and addiction. She became known as a pain management specialist, and consulted with several residential addiction treatment centers in the North Bay, and opened a private practice.

She redefined chronic pain, and now works with a process she created called, Prolonged Pain Complex, which she defines as a disorder of the mind, body, and spirit. Terrie has identified soft tissue impairment as one of the leading contributors to chronic pain, and this does not show up on X-rays or MRIs. It can only be evaluated through observation of an individual's movement patterns, and hands-on palpations of the strength and flexibility of the soft tissue. With the stimulus of pain, the soft tissue and fascia contract in a protective reaction, which is healthy. When that contraction continues over time, it causes joints to become compressed and wear out prematurely. This is a path to pain.

After an in-depth assessment process, she begins a three-level protocol:

- Reducing pain and quieting the central nervous system.
- Musculoskeletal rebalancing based on understanding kinesiology, or the science of movement.

- Strengthening and conditioning, which is the level at which most physical therapists begin.

Terri believes this protocol needs to be followed for healing to begin and to prevent further injuries.

Terrie is now in the third stage of her life and is ready to delegate more of the hands-on work with clients so she can move into a training and public speaking mode and take her business to a larger base of people. She believes the earlier she can reach people, the less pain they will have to endure. I wish I had met her at year one of my chronic pain rather than year four.

She's written two books, one just published this year called, *Hello, My Name is Pain,* which is available on Amazon. It's a short, easy to read book that explains how she treats physical, emotional, and spiritual pain. She believes the body, mind, and spirit must all be treated as an integrated whole, rather than as fractured entities with fragmented treatments. That's also why she often collaborates with psychotherapists and has a psychiatrist on her staff. Her first book, *Gathering Years: How to Grow Old Without Killing Yourself,* is an e-book available on her website, allies4change.com. She's enjoying this third stage of life, and has identified a successor in her business to take over daily operations while she focuses on growing the scale of her business.

She's had challenges to adapt to, and finds it can be difficult as a single woman to not feel lonely at times while aging without a significant other. At the same time, she feels very fulfilled in her career, her family, grandchildren, and her dance community. Terrie goes out many times a week swing dancing. In addition, she follows her own advice by staying fit with Pure Barre classes and going to the gym.

Terrie's suggestions for others are:

- Promote healing at the cellular level by following some simple daily practices—stay hydrated, eat small, frequent meals including protein, and move all your "real estate" every day, meaning all parts of your body.

- Develop a spiritual practice, or as she says, "eat spiritual foods," pray, meditate, experience and delight in anything that brings you pleasure.

- Find communities you can be part of to support you.

- Eliminate the idea that there's any shame in aging or experiencing pain.

- Recovery and healing is a process of change, and you need to be proactive, not passive, as we have been taught in our culture, when dealing with healthcare professionals.

- Pain medication and invasive surgeries can lead to addiction and weakened structures in the body, which make the soft tissue imbalance worse.

- Aging is not a chronic illness.

Chapter 6
An Inner Journey of Mindfulness and Spirituality

Most books on aging focus on exercise and diet as being critical to healthy aging, which of course they are. But, the total picture of successful aging needs to include inner as well as outer aging. As Lewis Richmond says in his book, *Aging as a Spiritual Practice,* inner and outer aging are close partners. In his description, inner aging includes serving others, being in nature, maintaining healthy relationships, and having an active spiritual life.

I find this to be true as I age, and I hear it also from my clients. I am more drawn to hiking and spending time in nature, embracing solitude and being mindful and grateful for each day. Before this time, I was too busy trying to get everything done at work and home, and rushing from one appointment to another, which didn't leave much time for quiet time and paying attention. Attention is the key to appreciating everything we have, even if we think what we have is not as much as we'd like. Staying focused on the present, paying attention, and developing gratitude for each day, each person, and all the small things, which really end up being the big things, is key to achieving your maximum level of satisfaction.

Avoid living in memories, good or bad. You can visit them for pleasure, but not dwell there for long periods, or you'll miss too much of what's happening right now that could be powerful. The present is the magic and the key to successful aging. It's important not to allow ourselves to fear or dread the future and the changes or physical decline it may bring. This gives too much power to the unknown and saps energy from today, and this is the only time we're sure we have.

Schedule days when you have nothing or very few things planned and can pay attention to what's happening below the surface when you are not busy distracting yourself. Turn inward to find your inner force, and ask for help from a divine power you personally believe in. Developing a spiritual practice can create powerful moments and bring learning, insights, and peace.

The book by Jack Kornfeld, *No Time Like the Present: Finding Freedom, Love, and Joy Right Where You Are,* emphasizes that outwardly you may be limited by the culture you live in, by an aging body, or the state of your finances. Yet there is a part of you that is your spirit, and it is always free to respond creatively.

Another book emphasizing the need for a spiritual life in this stage is *The Third Stage of Life*, by Daisaku Ikeda. He takes a Buddhist humanism approach toward aging, and has dedicated his life to a depth of spirit and purpose and commitment. He emphasizes the need to concentrate your entire being in each moment and in every encounter.

The work of Dr. Jon Kabat-Zinn who developed Mindfulness-Based Stress Reduction (MBSR), and wrote *Full Catastrophe Living*, has been helpful to me in coping with chronic pain. It doesn't eliminate the pain, but helps me relax into it, and gain ways of moving toward greater tolerance and self-compassion.

I've learned that I'm not my pain, and I'm separate from whatever is causing it. We need to learn that pain doesn't have anything to do with the essence of who we are. It's one thing to know this intellectually, but much harder to live it. I've also had to learn that "wanting" the pain to stop does not work, since wanting implies that I don't have it, and that it is dependent on something outside myself.

Finding a Joyful Life in the Heart of Pain by Darlene Cohen is another good resource for learning to live with pain.

Meditation is the form that many people use to become more reflective and relaxed, and this can bring relief of pain. While some people may not choose to formally meditate, "resting in awareness" as Lewis Richmond refers to it, will help relax our minds and let go of things as soon as they arise.

Aging with Attitude by Dr. Gerald Jampolsky and Diane Cirincione provides examples of how to live in this third stage of life by letting go of judgments, guilt, or anger because it is our own thoughts that cause us to feel fearful or upset. They apply the principles he has taught for decades at The Center for Attitudinal Healing in the San Francisco Bay Area and other global locations.

I would also recommend Richard Rohr's, book, *Falling Upward: A Spirituality for the Two Halves of Life.* I like the title since it's a great example of paradox, which he describes in his book as nondualistic thinking. Dualistic thinking is the pattern we use early in our life of knowing things by comparing them to others, and concluding one is good and therefore the opposite must be bad. In the first half of life, this polarity thinking may feel like it works. As we age, our frame of reference should become larger and more inclusive to welcome many seemingly opposing ideas. The goal is then to create wholeness and to see the whole and not just parts, as Rohr describes it. This allows us to fall upward and onward to a deeper and broader way of thinking. In this stage of life, we will experience losses. To be able to see the gains in them requires this much fuller way of thinking. At the same time, we need to focus in an inward way to find what is true for us individually. Again, a case of paradox thinking that can create more options.

Mindfulness is a topic related to this more expanded, and yet focused approach. Khurshed Dehnugara and Claire Genkai Breeze's book, *The Challenger Spirit,* uses mindfulness to help challenger leaders sustain their energy and performance to produce highly creative and pragmatic interventions. She uses neuroscience research to help people develop resistance and authentic leadership.

I find Claire's concepts useful in the third stage of life when resistance, resilience, and creativity are crucial in maintaining health, personal strength, and confidence. While her books are geared to working within organizations, the practices also apply to aging in our society. I especially like her term "aging disgracefully," which for us in the third stage of life means keeping our abilities to challenge and question the status quo, using our considerable experience as elders to mentor younger people who can become challengers, and taking part in social action to improve our current society.

I believe the older we become the more we have earned the right to make our opinions known, utilize our vision of how the world could function better, and make an impact. *The Power of Onlyness: Make Your Wild Ideas Mighty Enough to Dent the World* by Nilofer Merchant can help you activate your personal power to make more of a difference in the world. Her book will inspire you to find your purpose and join with others to create a common goal you all share to bring about major changes in the world. In this way, we can disrupt the approach that people in the third stage of their lives no longer have important work to contribute as elders and wise resources. Baby boomers and those who are coming after us are not going to go lightly into the third stage of life, but rather are going to make the most of their final years as elders and wise advocates for change. We all hope to change the world for the better, and enjoy ourselves along the way.

Exercises

What things could you give up doing to make time for more reflection and an inner focus to your life?

_____

_____

_____

How could you embrace a more expansive way of thinking to bring you fulfillment and empower yourself and others around you to create changes in their lives?

_____

_____

_____

How could you talk to yourself in a different way to bring yourself peace rather than discomfort and suffering?

_____

_____

_____

Interview

Kathy H. is a Principal with Harris and Simeone Consulting, and she began searching for an inner life before she was even in high school. She knew there was a powerful force within and all around her, which she wanted to explore and access. She began on the path of "always turning toward the light," as she says, to find life's true meaning. She started reading and studying spiritual works, such as *The Three Jewels,* which refers to the Buddhist teachings of the Buddha, Dharma, and Sangha. Through different teachings such as *The Work of Byron Katie,* the teachings of J. Krishnamurti, and the *Course in Miracles*, she discovered tools to investigate one's thoughts and stories that create suffering, and ways to explore one's true nature. She emphasizes peace is possible regardless of your situation, and you are not a victim.

She says, "Difficult circumstances in your life are catalysts for your development. When you take one step toward the Divine, it takes a thousand steps toward you."

She facilitated two-hour sessions with prisoners at San Quentin for 12 years to help them connect with their inner lives. She led two groups of men—one group who was eligible for parole, and a second group who was in prison for life. By not having resources for external lives, they were supported in opening to inner freedom. The men learned to develop vibrant inner lives, and she now works individually with some of them who are on parole.

She also worked at The Center for Attitudinal Healing facilitating groups, and now sees individual clients and groups at her home.

She makes annual backpacking trips to Yosemite, and strongly believes in the power of nature, and next year plans to take a group of prison parolees with her.

She works with patients at the Stanford protocol, a Stanford affiliate, and facilitates corporate groups on Communications Skills and Team Development.

She emphasizes we all need to decide where to put our focus and allegiance. Is it to acquiring things and status, or to inner freedom? Suffering, transitions, and change have a way of bringing us to the need to do inner work. Retirement and the third stage of life can be the catalyst to begin this vital work.

She recommends the work of Byron Katie, Eckhart Tolle, Rumi, Hafiz, and J. Krishnamurti.

Kathy's suggestions for others are:

- Connect to your inner force because we are all seeking inner peace.
- Embrace your true inner nature rather than being only outwardly driven.
- Find what's alive for you. Meet and feel any additional emotions, including resistance.

- Read and attend courses at places like Spirit Rock in the San Francisco Bay Area, or other spiritual centers in your community. Work with others, a group, or a teacher who can inspire you to begin on this path.

- Get clear on what your identity is and where your allegiance lies.

Chapter 7
Connections to Others

Making an impact has always been important to me, as it is to most human beings. We don't want to think we've lived our lives and not made a difference to any person or organization. Fortunately, most people make much more of an impact than they realize, especially at this stage of their lives when they have wisdom and time to share it.

Challenging yourself to learn new things, give back to the community, and meet new people are critical parts of having a satisfying and meaningful third stage of life. Find ways to give what you know to others, or give the gift of your time to make a personal connection. Mentor others and be conscious of how your behavior at this stage of life impacts younger people and all who observe you. This is harder to do if you're not regularly in contact with people as you used to be at work. However, many people have churches they attend, friends they could see more regularly, or new organizations ready to welcome their volunteer time.

I recently joined a nonprofit philanthropy organization created by women to fund other nonprofit organizations. Given the reduction to nonprofit funding and grants no longer being available in the government budget, it seems especially important to me to help fund these organizations in our communities.

I also know of several volunteer jobs that have turned into paying activities for some of my clients. I think it's very satisfying, and often necessary, to earn money in your third stage of life. Many people have expertise they can use in consulting or teaching, and finding even a few clients can give you a sense of purpose and increase your personal contacts.

Create a Deeper Connection with Your Partner

If you are fortunate enough to have a partner at this stage in life, it's the perfect time to focus on this relationship and solidify it in an even stronger way. Many people become so involved with their families or work that their partners are often overlooked or taken for granted, especially if they've been together for many years. I can't pass up this opportunity to say that having Michael as my husband for so many years is my "secret sauce," and I am his. Without each other to spend time with and go through the ups and downs of life, it would be a much lonelier trip.

But, I hear from others they've become disconnected from their partner of many years. Now is the perfect time to rediscover one another and make each other a top priority in your lives. A satisfying partnership brings tremendous joy to aging. You can look to the other person as a source of fun, companionship, advocacy, and intimacy.

I was trying to decide where to put sexuality in these chapters, and I think it belongs here since it's one of the most profound ways to make a personal connection with others at this stage in your life. Many people tell me they have become more sexual with partners at this stage in their lives because they have the time to focus on it, and have come to appreciate the love they have for the other person. Not to mention it's fun and free! Creativity is the name of the game here since you may not function in the same way sexually as you did when you were younger. But, this just means you can try new things. Experimentation is part of the fun if both parties can agree on what's enjoyable.

For those who don't have a regular partner, it may be time to start looking for opportunities to be physically close to another person, whether it's someone you want around all the time or not. Intimacy is a calming gift and gratifying when you can give it or receive it. Touch itself is something many people lament losing when their past partner dies or leaves. Holding, touching, kissing, closeness, massage is very satisfying and could stop there, or turn into something more sexual depending on your preference. Just don't stop doing it. Don't stop trying to be close just because your bodies have changed and you may have some inner messages that tell you to stop such behavior "at your age." Communicate with each other and decide what's fun to do and do it. There should be no judgment about how things used to be or what anyone else might think. Many people tell me this stage of life offers the best sex they've had at any time in their lives. Partnership and love can be more important now than at any other time.

Finding new friends and activities is important to stretch your thinking and provide new companionship. Loneliness can be challenging for single people at this stage of their lives. Staying in touch with old friends and contributing your expertise to the community can make your life have purpose and keep you from feeling lonely. Solitude is enriching and nurturing, and shouldn't be confused with being lonely.

Grandchildren and Children

Most people who have grandchildren will tell you this is one of the most important and satisfying relationships in their lives. Modeling conscious living for grandchildren and the pure joy of just having fun with them will keep you fully in the present and growing and changing every day, along with their growth. Now is also the time of growth with your children, if you have them. There is a closeness you can have with adult children that is very special and much different than you may have had when you were raising them. Going out together, being friends, and learning from them just as they have learned from you is a fascinating dynamic. If you haven't had children, you can do this with a godchild or any child who's a friend of your family or someone new you meet. Part of leaving a legacy is helping to develop a younger person. However you choose to do that, you'll find it is satisfying and a gift for both parties.

Exercises

How can you find new ways to be close to someone you are partnered with? Are the two of you in agreement about how to spend these retirement years?

_____

_____

_____

How can you connect with friends to revitalize relationships that may not have received much attention recently? Where can you meet new friends?

_____

_____

_____

How can you find organizations to provide new contacts and challenge yourself more?

_____

_____

_____

Interview

It can often be difficult for people with senior level positions and successful careers to be ready to retire and move on to new things. Dick F. had the opposite experience.

Now 80, he had retired 20 years ago at the age of 60, moved across the country with his wife, and has enjoyed creating new opportunities including civic and volunteer experiences.

Early in his career, he received an MBA from Cornell in Marketing when it was still unusual for people to get MBAs, and he was recruited to Procter & Gamble, an ideal place to learn brand management and packaged goods. After four years, he left to join an advertising agency in San Francisco, and later was recruited to Hunt Wesson and then Land-O-Lakes as an EVP. After leaving to take an equity role in another company that required him to spend full weeks in Chicago and commute home to Minnesota on the weekends, he decided he'd had enough corporate life and was ready for new adventures.

He says one of the most important factors in making retirement successful for him is that he and his wife of 51 years have always been on the same page about what they wanted. He says he never could have relocated across the country several times and planned this stage of his life if they had not agreed together on the next steps.

They made a checklist of what was most important to them, and decided they wanted to move to a new location in a smaller town with good weather outside a larger city. Since they had lived in San Francisco earlier in his career, they decided to try the wine country an hour north of there. The town of Sonoma ended up being a perfect fit for them where they built a house a block from town on a cul-de-sac to give them privacy and quick access to the square.

He and his wife have both been very active in local and county civic ventures. He still works on the board of directors of an insurance company, and volunteers at local retirement communities. He and his wife both have many connections in the community, and she referred me to the nonprofit philanthropy organization I became a member of.

He's in good health, but had several knee surgeries after years of running, and is now slowing down and focusing on eating in a healthy way. He goes to the gym five to six hours a week, and he and his wife travel regularly, recently returning from a trip back to see friends in Minnesota.

He and his wife have both continued to make new friends, as well as focus on each other, their family, and community.

Dick's suggestions for others are:

- Know yourself and what will be satisfying to you, and don't get too tied up in your work.
- Have a sense of purpose, and if you're single, pick your partner carefully since that will help determine how satisfying these final years can be.
- Get involved in your community and meet new people.
- Keep things in perspective and take pride in a job well done, while at the same time challenging yourself to learn new things.
- Establish a balanced focus on health and your finances, since having one without the other will not provide a satisfying third stage of life.

Chapter 8
Time Is the New Money

Financial advisors tell you to keep working if you can so you're sure you have enough money to retire. Many of them have caused people to think they can never afford to quit working full time. I suggest the opposite. I think you should quit working for others as soon as you feel completed with your job, have some savings and are ready to move on.

I'm not suggesting you don't save enough money to live on in your retirement, but this doesn't mean you need to live exactly the way you are today, if you're willing to try something new.

Experiences are the things you need more of, and you're not going to get those from staying longer in the same job, unless you're always taking on new responsibilities and learning new things. You may be at an organization that lets you try out new positions every few years and continues to challenge you. If so, that's great, and you may want to ride it out for a while, but that's rare.

Opt for time over money, and force yourself out of your comfort zone. Give yourself permission to try something new, live somewhere new, or study something new. This time in your life is your last chance to mix it up. We're not one-dimensional people who are meant to keep doing only one thing, work constantly, and never take breaks. Even if you think the trade-off is a paycheck that you can't imagine doing without, think about what else you could be missing.

I'm not suggesting you stop supporting yourself or your family or quit without having enough money to live on. But, once you've saved whatever amount you can get comfortable with, move on. You will probably still earn more in this third stage of life, and you can likely get another job if you choose to, or create your own business.

I know this runs counter to what we've been told, especially baby boomers. But, millennials will tell you that it's not all about the job. It's about the learning, the experiences, and your life that you need to focus on. Unfortunately, many people don't think of time as an asset. Some are addicted to their jobs, think they have no purpose without them, and our society reinforces that focus.

Valuing your time can be as basic as learning to say "no" to things others ask of you that don't sound interesting, to organizing your home office, to eliminating the paperwork clutter slowing you down and making simple jobs more complicated.

The challenge is to change your mindset to value your time and monitor how you're using it to make the impact you desire.

Since many people seek help from accountants or financial advisors on the topic of money management in the third stage of life, I almost didn't bother to include a chapter on this topic. But, because it's such an important area I decided it had to be in here, especially in a more provocative way that discusses valuing time over money.

This is an area where being innovative and exploring new ways of living can be very important and satisfying, although the idea of downsizing financially can be threatening for many people. I'm not a financial advisor, so I won't attempt to give technical advice. But, I will talk about things that have worked for me and for some of my clients. Many people haven't started early enough to work out a retirement budget for this stage of their lives. You probably thought I was going to say they haven't started saving soon enough, but everyone knows we all could have probably done better on that point.

Saving is difficult when you have debt to pay off, a family to raise, children in college or even just yourself to support when the costs of housing, healthcare and basic living expenses continue to rise faster than wages. People who have worked their entire lives can reach retirement with little savings to supplement the meager amount from Social Security and few pensions are available. But, the resource they still have is time to enjoy themselves and make changes in their lifestyles.

Several years before stopping full-time work, you can begin projecting the level of savings you will have based on your current saving levels and spending. Since housing is often a large part of the budget, if you haven't paid off a mortgage or are renting, you may want to explore buying or renting a smaller home than the one you have now. You will most likely want to do that while you're still employed so you can qualify for the best mortgage, if you need one, or look acceptable on a rental application. If you want to stay in the same general location, but might consider a different house or condo, meet with a real estate agent who can register you for one of the agent-sponsored websites so you'll see properties immediately when they come on the MLS. If you're buying, work with an agent who can tell you about pocket listings that aren't on the market yet.

This is how we found the home we plan to live in for the third stage of our lives since it was soon to be put on the market. It was a pocket listing our agent received right before we were going to make an offer on another house. We were thankful we found out about this listing that wasn't on the market yet because it had many features that were a better fit for what we wanted, and it was in a better location. If we had tried to buy it after it was listed, we know we would have been in a bidding war with others since we live in a hot real estate area, and that would have made it too expensive for our budget.

We made our new home into a vacation rental until we were ready to move into it full time, because it's too far a commute for me while still working in San Francisco. Since this new area is where we wanted to live after I had a more flexible work schedule, we knew the sooner we could get into the market the less expensive it would be.

Friends and clients of mine have also been successful in moving, at least for part of the year, to a location with a cheaper cost of living. Mexico, South America, parts of both Western and Eastern Europe, and Asia all have desirable locations that are far cheaper than many places in the United States, while still having good and more reasonable medical care and many English-speaking expats.

Malaysia, France, and Costa Rica are all known for their good healthcare options. Medical tourism is also becoming popular for those who choose not to pay for expensive medical procedures in the United States.

For people willing to be adventurous, considering new locations for living part of the year, if not full time, can be a viable option for cutting expenses in half, or more. It also offers the chance to learn new things, experience different cultures, and meet new people, all of which are exciting and healthy in the third stage of your life. Seniornomads.com is an example of a couple in their 60s who have been traveling for the last four years, staying for months at a time at Airbnbs. They are leading an adventurous life, negotiated an internship with Airbnb and wrote a book about their experiences.

International Living is a good publication to give you more exposure to different locations (InternationalLiving.com). In their January 2017 issue, they list Mexico as the #1 retirement destination in their Global Retirement Index. This is the fifth year Mexico has taken the top spot. Due to affordability, being conveniently close to the United States, having good healthcare, friendly locals and expats, and a low peso currently makes it a bargain. Many locations stand out, such as San Miguel de Allende, where we just returned from, Puerto Vallarta, Playa del Carmen, Tulum, Merida, Lake Chapala, and Guanajuato, to mention a few.

Having access to Mayan culture, low cost for food and housing, and good internet access is a plus. IL also sponsors tours to research countries, such as Belize, Panama, and Ecuador, and IL publishes books written by people who have relocated to other countries.

Working part-time in consulting, teaching, technology, or other areas to supplement your savings and Social Security helps. It keeps you involved in an area you hopefully enjoy, forces you to keep learning new things, and makes your money last longer.

While you're still working and planning for the third stage of life, I recommend the next position you take be one you can eventually do as an entrepreneur or part-time when you choose to make the move to retirement. Better still would be if it can be done virtually at least part of the time to allow for travel or relocation.

Travel doesn't have to be expensive if you're using airline miles or going to less expensive places to live than where you live during the rest of the year. If you are comfortable renting out your home for part or all of the time you're gone, or exchanging it, this will help offset expenses. I also know people who do housesitting and pet sitting all over the world as an inexpensive way to travel without paying for hotels.

Worrying about expenses is frustrating, and I'd suggest reducing your expenses as soon as possible, or increasing your income to help you enjoy these final 20 to 30-plus years. This could likely mean a change in where you live now or the lifestyle you currently enjoy. But, change is the one constant you can count on at this stage, and the sooner you can embrace it the better. A change in scenery and a new group of people or exposure to a new culture and language can be the best thing at this stage of life to increase your neurons and forge new pathways in the brain. You can also find reasonably priced and interesting places to live in the United States if you're not interested in living in another country.

If you're going to retire in your current home, you'll need to plan for who can help you maintain the home when you're not physically up to it, and this may include making some modifications to your home. You will also eventually need someone who can become a healthcare worker for you when you need physical and medical help, or organizations to drive you to appointments.

I also suggest that you be directly involved in managing your finances, if you have an interest in it, rather than paying a sizeable sum to have investment advisors do it for you. Again, that's probably the opposite of what you'd hear from your accountant or attorney.

If you can invest in Index funds that mirror the S&P 500, you'll likely have as good a return as managed accounts, especially if you add individual stocks you've researched that pay dividends or are growth stocks. There are many newsletters and publications you can subscribe to that can help you select funds, and suggest when to make moves in the market.

People in retirement are often advised to have a high percentage of bonds in their portfolio for lower risk, but the returns are often too low to maximize your nest egg. There are countless other Index funds such as those that mirror the small cap Russell 2000 that can be more aggressive, and international stocks if you have a comfort level with that amount of risk for a portion of your money. As I'm writing this, global markets are doing even better than the United States, and in 2017 we're having strong stock market performance. The reward is often worth it if you have a personal interest, risk tolerance, and a desire to pay attention to the state of the market. If this doesn't interest you, find someone you trust to manage your money.

My husband and I have "money meetings," as we call them, once every few weeks, usually on Saturday mornings. We discuss our portfolio and enjoy exploring new investments, or deciding whether it's time to sell ones we currently have. We watch financial shows like *Fast Money* on CNBC and read books to better educate ourselves, because this nest egg is what we need to live on for the next 25-plus years, so who should be more interested in paying attention to it than us? My husband learned to become a conservative options trader (which is probably another paradox), and he really enjoys it and makes money without taking large risks.

This may not be right for everyone, but paying percentage points to others to possibly do less of a good job than we've done ourselves over the past 20 years is not appealing to us. We've interviewed several people who wanted us to take a conservative approach to investing because we are in our 60s. That may be the correct approach for some people, but it's not the right one for us.

Decide for yourself how you want your money managed, by you or someone else, and don't let anyone talk you into doing something that's comfortable for them but not you.

Exercises

Is it possible for you to quit your current job if you're not learning anything new and explore other options?

_____

_____

_____

If so, what else would you consider doing either full time or part time?

_____

_____

_____

Would it be on option to leave your position and retire earlier than you anticipated if you downsized, or considered other ways to increase your income?

_____

_____

_____

Is there another location you would consider relocating to, even for a short period of time, to save money? If so, for how long and what places interest you?

_____

_____

_____

What kind of part-time work would you consider, such as consulting, teaching, writing, TaskRabbit work, or any work that could bring additional money or better benefits than Medicare, Social Security, or a pension?

_____

_____

_____

Interview

Arden H. was a past client of mine years ago, and is a current client again today. She is an excellent example of someone who knows the value of time and manages it well. She also manages her household's money. She owns a successful business as an interior designer, and utilizes her time very effectively. She is now exploring the next business she wants to open, if she decides to reduce the amount of time she spends in her current business.

She says she learned very early to value time and manage it well when she was in school and was elected president of a social club and needed to schedule many activities. The teacher who worked with this group gave her a system and suggestions for how to efficiently use her time and balance this with her other work at school. It was the first time she had thought of the need to value her time and considered ways to manage it more effectively.

Arden began to appreciate time even more when she was involved in a life-threatening car accident at age 19. It made her realize how quickly things can change and the time you thought you'd have in the future could easily go away. This caused her to become much less scattered in how she used her time, and more focused and determined to spend her time well on healing. She realized her life was in her hands, and it also helped her to learn to set goals, read books on time management, and start seeing time as an asset. She began to compartmentalize things and take nothing for granted.

After deciding to move from Portland, Oregon, to San Francisco, she wanted to start her own business. This decision caused her to become even more aware of the need to value her time because she now had many more things to do than when she was working for someone else.

Now that she has owned a very successful interior design business for many years, she attributes her ability to focus and effectively manage her time as keys to success. At the age of 67, she is thoughtful about how she spends her time because she is starting to feel her energy level may not be the same as it was years before, and she prioritizes the most important things to accomplish in a day. She's now more realistic about how many things can be done at once, and paces herself to work at this rapid pace for a few more years. She enjoys working, and we are exploring possibilities for an additional business, if she chooses to cut back the time she spends on her current business to free up some time.

She also manages her family's money well, and learned this from her father who had a background in economics. He taught her about the importance of saving and investing.

She and her husband have different approaches to money, and they have regular discussions about how to be on the same page regarding money for their retirement. She subscribes to financial newsletters, manages their portfolio of stocks, and reads books on money management.

When she cuts back on work in her retirement, she says she's looking forward to having more time to manage their money.

There are very few things she would do differently about either time or money if she was in her 20s or 30s and just starting out. But, the one thing she would have done is to find a way to get more involved in real estate investing. She wished she would have bought Victorian houses in San Francisco when she was younger, but thought she didn't have the money. Now she knows there are many ways to find money if you're willing to think outside the box, be creative, and take some well-thought-out risks.

Arden's suggestions for others are:

- Value your time and make the best use of it. You never know when it could be taken away.

- Take care of your body and invest in keeping it healthy.

- Don't wait to do things if your intuition tells you something is the right thing to do.

- In your retirement, look for ways to increase your income and review your expenses. But, first look for opportunities for growth since there are many ways to work part-time to supplement your savings.

- Don't be resistant to learning about money. Realize it can give you freedom and control over your life, and allow you to always be able to rely on yourself.

Chapter 9
Creative Growth Activities

Finding new creative activities to engage in increases brain growth and brings relaxation and pleasure. As I mentioned earlier, calming the central nervous system is key to maintaining health and minimizing stress. Physically engaging in a new creative process builds new pathways in the brain, increases neurons, calms the central nervous system, and is fun!

Many people think they're not creative or artistic, but generally I've found that most people are to a certain degree. They simply haven't had the time or opportunity to discover what areas could be most satisfying to them. As children, we were creative and regularly made things with our hands, sang, played an instrument, drew pictures, and danced. We let go of many of those things as adults because we began evaluating how good we were at them, and usually found we did not measure up to our expectations. We also didn't have time to pursue them because more important things such as our career or raising children became priorities.

The third stage of life is focused on removing judgment and doing things for fulfillment, pleasure, and purpose. This is a time to free ourselves from our own or anyone else's evaluation and experiment with new things. It doesn't matter how good we are at creating something; it matters that we use our brain in new ways to keep it healthy and growing, and that we enjoy our life.

I've never known how to draw, and in my third stage of life I told myself that I would start to sketch and paint. I'm now taking a class in drawing, and there are many on YouTube that are interesting. These classes have me sketching things I never would have attempted before.

My neighbor does oil painting in his 80s, and a woman I know who has painted for years is now serious enough about it to display her work at a local gallery. The result of your creative venture doesn't matter. It's the process and learning that's important.

Many people try writing for the first time. I've never written a book but always wanted to for my own fulfillment, and to share some of my thoughts with others to help them during this transition to the third stage of their lives. I thought it could be useful for my clients, it's enjoyable for me, and hopefully will help others disrupt their current thinking about retirement and aging and try something new.

An enjoyable book to read that presents 10 principles to help you discover your artistic side and build a more creative nature is *Steal Like an Artist*, by Austin Kleon. It's inspiring, brief, and easy to read. He follows his own advice that "creativity is subtraction," and in our culture of overload, placing limitations on yourself can help you become free to do your best work. Another paradoxical idea, I know, but I believe it's true. I have found in writing this book that what you leave out is just as important as what you put in. And writing less is harder than writing more.

Another book I'd recommend for connecting with your creativity is *The Art of Creative Thinking*, by Rod Judkins. He covers 89 ways to see things differently, which ties in again with my enjoyment of paradox. These are things that turn conventional thinking on its head, and get you to look at the world with fresh eyes. Curiosity and openness, as he says, are two of the most important attributes for someone in the third stage of life. These can help you come alive and discover new worlds.

Travel can stimulate your creativity, especially if you do it in a different way than you have the rest of your life, or go to totally new places. The role of the creative person is to disturb, question, and unsettle. We can do things we've done before, and still be creative by approaching them in a new way.

Exercises

What one or two things could you learn to do that would bring you creative pleasure? Have you tried things in the past that you could get back to if you have more time?

_____

_____

_____

Is there a role model you can think of who has brought creativity into his or her life in this third stage? What things have they done that could apply to you?

_____

_____

_____

Interview

Kayla C. retired at age 66 from a career as a psychiatrist in private practice. She gave her clients a year's notice prior to making the move. Her planning and discussions with her husband were helpful, and she knew she was ready. She said she was meticulous about how she dismantled her office, and has no regrets about leaving her practice. She feels good about herself and the life and career she has led. She believes having this closure has been a key factor in the satisfaction she feels about being retired.

After a brief period of reflection when it became clear to her that she was replaceable in her client's lives, she decided this was a good thing, and since then has felt very happy to be in an active retirement. She has challenges, such as having diabetes for years, and is managing that physical challenge very well.

She took an initial trip to Eastern Europe to celebrate her retirement, and planned to spend time with her aging mother after she returned. Unfortunately, her mother died suddenly three weeks after her return from the trip. Although she still feels she is grieving the loss of her mother, she is now finding purpose and satisfaction from a variety of activities. These include taking her volunteer dog to two hospitals each week to work with the patients, to remodeling her kitchen and planning future trips to Eastern Europe. One way she expresses her creativity is through travel, and her goal is to eventually become an expat for a year by renting out her house and relocating temporarily. She could imagine herself working abroad either teaching English or working as a tour guide. She loves travel and hopes to do more of it in the future. She's a voracious reader, and is involved in gardening and cultural activities. She also has a creative outlet making jewelry with a group of other therapists who periodically get together.

She is an introvert and is happy to be less involved with the external world. She is relieved to feel less attached to what others think and to focus on her own interests. She said the only thing she might do differently in hindsight would be to retire sooner, giving her clients a six-month notice instead of a year. Other than that, she is very satisfied and has adjusted well to her new lifestyle.

Kayla's suggestions for others are:

- Recognize the importance of planning and gaining closure so you can feel positive about the career and life you've had up to this point.
- Enjoy yourself and find a variety of creative interests to make you feel you're using your skills and time well.
- Don't hesitate to be adventurous about changing your life to include new places and new activities. It's fun and good for the brain to get those neurons stimulated.

Chapter 10
Your Legacy and Completion of Life

I don't know if anyone can do a better job of describing this phase of life than Angeles Arrien did in her book, *The Second Half of Life*. In her chapter, "The Gold Gate," she discusses nonattachment, surrender, and letting go. Closure is the critical step in this final part of the process as it will bring us to the completion and release of everything in our lives, and cause us to have no regrets. At this stage, we try to learn to befriend death and to make peace with everything and everyone around us.

The most important legacy we can leave is the belief that life is and has been worthwhile, right up to the end. How a person meets death is a sign of how they have met life. This may be the greatest model we can leave to our family and friends.

Write down what legacies are important for you to share with your children, friends, or partners. Ask them what were the most important things they'll remember about you. What have you learned from each other? Candid conversation is so important at the end of your life and is often hard to get from your loved ones, since they may feel awkward talking about the topic, or feel a need to say, "Oh, you'll be around for years, so let's don't talk about that now."

I've written a document for our son called "Family Milestones" that covers all the key things we've done in our three lives and when we did them so he'll be able to remember these things when both my husband and I are gone. He doesn't remember some of the early things that happened before he was eight years of age, and he can refer to this document whenever he needs or wants.

You may also want to give away certain personal items to people while you're still healthy so you can experience the enjoyment they receive from them, and know your wishes for who will receive what will be honored. I intend to do this with many of my things and have designated certain items for family and friends.

Where will you be buried, or will you be cremated? Have you expressed your wishes to your loved ones? Do you want a funeral or a different type of celebration of life? Or nothing at all? Who do you want with you in your final hours? Is your will prepared so relatives will not do things that would be contrary to your wishes? Do you have an executor/executrix of your will? Answer these questions in addition to those below.

Meg Newhouse's book, *Legacies of the Heart*, can give you additional ideas about the keys to legacy living, and she tells many stories of people who have left impactful legacies for their loved ones.

For those who have enough funds to provide for yourself and your loved ones, you may want to consider philanthropy and donate an amount of your estate to a foundation or causes you believe in. Philanthropic advisors can create plans for you and advise you on non-profit groups or foundations to consider. It doesn't need to be a lot of money to make an impact. As one man I interviewed did, you can set up a scholarship for $5,000 that could make a difference to a student struggling to afford additional schooling. There are tax benefits to making these types of charitable donations that can also be helpful, but most people seem compelled to do this more from a desire to give back and see the money they have earned make an impact on others.

I plan to write what Ron Pevny in his book, *Conscious Living, Conscious Aging*, calls a legacy letter to several people describing my unique life journey, and expressing my feelings for them.

I've also been writing journals since I was 25, and I have a collection of them in case my son or my husband want to read them if I die before they do. I enjoy writing them, and they may find them interesting, or not. Either way, they help me process my thinking and work through issues, and I feel better that I've left them some written history. Videos are an easy way to do this now that everyone has phones that take videos. These will be engaging for family and friends to see after you or your loved ones are gone. Conversations with people you care about are so important to have as they and you are aging.

I wish I had the opportunity to do this with my parents when they were alive. My father died suddenly from a heart attack when I was 25 so there was no time to think about getting closure with him as it was so unexpected. I would have liked to have told him because of the way he lived his life and respected and loved my mother that I had a model of what to look for in the man I married. Michael, my husband, is like my father in many ways, and without both of us seeing the partnership my parents had, we would not have the heartfelt relationship we have today.

My mother died at 74 of cancer, but prior to that she had a stroke, which made it very difficult for her to talk. I attempted to record a discussion with her, but she couldn't have a dialogue and it ended up being me talking and her listening. Hopefully, it still made a difference to her that I wanted to do it. She was my role model and helped me become the woman I am today. My husband, sister, and I were with her when she died, and I am so happy to have had that experience. Don't wait too long to have these kinds of conversations with people you love.

Exercises

What do you want your legacy to be?

_____

_____

_____

What can you do now to leave something memorable for your friends and family?

_____

_____

_____

If you knew you were dying in the next six months, what would you do differently?

_____

_____

_____

Could you be doing some of these things now?

_____

_____

_____

Interview

Bette, at the age of 89, is still in good health, and because she's a very organized person, she's also taken care of many things to provide closure and completion for her life.

She had a long career as a teacher and social worker/therapist, and was still teaching art at the Teacher's College at Columbia University in her 70s. She taught at all levels from kindergarten, junior high, high school, and then moved on to college level as an art teacher. She also taught overseas in France and England for four years.

During this third stage of her life, she has continued to find enjoyment doing her art, reading, walking, meditating, exercising, and visiting friends. She used to volunteer at the Whistlestop, an organization to assist people who are aging with transportation, meal delivery, and other services. She began a women's group called Namaste, and has attended groups at Spirit Rock.

She has taken care of all the details of planning for her death and selecting an executrix for her will. She has given away many of her artworks, furniture, and other things over the past several years to people who can enjoy them. She has also written letters to various friends to express her feelings for them.

She did not have her own children, but is the godmother of two daughters of a former student of hers who has become a good friend. She also has a niece with two children. She says all her friends are younger than she is, and teaching has kept her involved with younger people during her life.

She has always had an active inner life, and this has increased in her later years. She is living a healthy and satisfying third stage of life.

Bette's recommendations for others are:

- Maintain friendships that nourish you, and do not spend time with people you don't really enjoy. Learn to say "no" and set limits on how you want to spend your time.
- Develop an interest that is creative, whether it is art or music or anything that will bring a spark of creativity to your life.
- Let go of things that are not important in your life and get down to the essentials.
- Develop a "spine of connection that supports your inner growth." A spiritual practice is especially important at this stage in life when your focus is less on the outer world. Find a spiritual teacher if you have not been involved with meditation and spiritual practices in the past.

Summary

I learned many things while writing this book, and it confirmed some I suspected were true. Many may seem obvious and some may seem repetitive, but all are important parts of the transition for the people I interviewed.

The key points I heard in my interviews were:

- Planning for the third stage of life is critical, and can make the transition much simpler and more productive. Nevertheless, I had one interviewee who took the opposite approach because he is comfortable with paradox thinking, and likes doing the opposite of what might seem to be the obvious way. He dislikes planning and believes that the right approach for him is to let things evolve, provided he doesn't have high expectations that things will always work out or be perfect.

- It's not only the privileged who can have a satisfying retirement. While it helps to have a certain amount of money and somewhat good health to have a satisfying aging process, I talked to countless people who are doing it on less of both of those things. They are changing their lives so they can live on less, often in a new, cheaper location, or they're working at least part time to afford the lifestyle they choose. The people who are most satisfied with doing this are those who see it as an adventure and not something to be fearful of, because that saps the energy out of every day.

• Your relationships are key, especially with your partner, closest friends, and community, and you can still start new relationships with people of all ages in your 70s and 80s that will bring you great satisfaction and provide new thinking.

• The most important relationship is still with yourself, and you need to dedicate time to nurturing it. Look to yourself for guidance. The more you care for your body, mind, soul, heart, and spirit that make up the essence of your identity, the better your third stage of life will be, and the more you will have to offer others.

• Men and women often have different approaches to retirement and the third stage of life. Men (or women) whose primary identities have been their careers often have a harder time finding other options to consider. Women (or men) who've been raising families and haven't been focused on their careers are often now ready to get more work focused. Some couples may find one member is gearing up while the other is gearing down. Men also seem to become more comfortable with their emotional and spiritual side as they age, and become more playful and at ease with their grandchildren than they had time to be with their children. It was much easier for the women I interviewed to be creative and come up with many options for how to spend their time and deal with ambiguity.

• Creative ventures live in all of us if we take time to develop them. These will give us satisfaction at this stage of our lives, reduce stress, and feed our minds. We need to use a broad definition of what *creative* means— it could be art, music, adventure, travel, or a new cause to be passionate about.

• Philanthropy and leaving a legacy, financial or personal, can be satisfying processes and bring closure to our lives.

• The more we remove fear from this stage of our life and substitute confidence, fun, and satisfaction with what we have accomplished and can still accomplish, the better our remaining years will be.

• Pursuing entrepreneurial activities can be the most satisfying and lucrative way to work at this stage. Even if you never thought you'd work on your own or start a business, now can be the time. Start simple, think big. Decide to intentionally keep it small. Be satisfied with the new things that develop. If you already have a business, consider how you'd like to change it to be more fulfilling and a better fit for this stage of your life.

- Change is your mantra, and something you must become comfortable with if you want a satisfying third stage. Health, finances, friends all change, and you need to take time to grieve their passing, but then move on and make something positive of the change. This won't be easy, and it takes time.

- Don't listen to anyone but yourself, and do the things that feel right to you.

- Develop an internal life in addition to an external life. Learn to meditate, enjoy solitude, nature, and free time. Live in the present with a feeling of gratitude. A spiritual practice is especially important in this later stage of life when your focus moves away from external activities.

- Don't give away your time unless the activity sounds interesting and you can learn something from it. Only spend time with people who enrich you. Set boundaries and focus on things deserving of the time you have left.

- Be a disrupter of what many people think this last stage of life is all about. Model for younger people the best is yet to come. Don't let anyone cause you to feel diminished or declining because of your age. Be proud of the age you are, and let everyone know it. Use your gifts to contribute to the world and your wisdom to act as an elder. How else can we change society's negative attitude about people in the third stage of their lives? Fight ageism at every opportunity.

- Feel satisfied and finished with the past, stay focused on the present, and be excited about what could happen in the future. But, don't be a Pollyanna and think that everything will turn out perfect. As one person told me, his 92-year-old mother said on her deathbed, "Why me?!" It's going to end at some point, things aren't all going to go well, and that's just life. Try to make the end of your life a conscious death, as you have tried to live a conscious life.

Epilogue

I started writing this book the first day of my retirement, and I'm ending it one year later. How do I feel about things now that my retirement has reached its first anniversary? Overall, I feel satisfied with this first year. I can't believe the time has gone by so quickly, and both my husband and I agree it's been one of the best years of our lives. I think the reason we feel this way is the combination of time and freedom, doing things that give both of us a sense of purpose, and having more time to spend together and on a variety of activities we enjoy. This doesn't mean it was an easy trip, and at times I felt overwhelmed with the transition.

I created a new identity for myself, combining work I had always done as a coach, counselor, and consultant with other things I had done for fun in the past. I'm now primarily a coach/consultant, designer, and writer. I started and grew my coaching and consulting practice, and work with clients individually who are either in the third stage of life or planning for it, who currently range in age from 52 to 74. I work several days a week doing this, and really enjoy my clients, and the progress I see them making.

I spent time focusing on my health, and am feeling much better and stronger than I did a year ago. This will continue to be an ongoing focus for me and my husband, because we want to age in a healthy way.

I started my jewelry design and consulting business to develop my creative side, and have individual clients I've redesigned jewelry for that they were not wearing and wanted to recycle. I've also designed new jewelry they wanted to make as part of their creative processes. I've even recycled a few pieces for myself along the way. Sustainability should apply to everything, including jewelry. If you're not wearing it and enjoying it, give it away, sell it to someone, or redesign and recycle it.

I've also held jewelry trunk shows, which have been successful and fun. I've sold pieces from my personal collection, and from new artists I met this year. I plan to do more of these shows next year.

We spent more time at our vacation rental home where we'll eventually move, and are gradually getting our current home ready to sell at some point in the future.

We took a trip to San Miguel de Allende, Mexico when I first retired for my birthday, and it had been 40 years since we went there the last time for my birthday! It's a great town we really enjoyed. We met new friends and found a new artist whose pieces I've sold.

We also took a trip with our son, daughter-in-law, and grandson, invited my sister and her husband to our house for a week, as well as other friends of ours. We've had time to socialize more, and we never seemed to have enough time to do this before.

I joined a women's nonprofit philanthropy organization. They fund nonprofit organizations in Sonoma County, and I plan to get more involved in it this year.

I spent more time managing our money with my husband. We've had fun doing it, and it's produced some good results. It's the only way we'll have enough to last our lifetime. Fortunately, it's been a good year for the stock market.

I'm taking a drawing class so I can eventually paint. This will be an ongoing learning activity.

I've developed a more active spiritual practice. I've read and studied about my inner life, and I want to nurture this part of my identity. I now believe everything that matters is "in here," not "out there," and I have no interest in controlling myself or others, which is the operating system of the ego.

I finished writing this book, which took a lot of time and research and feels like a major accomplishment! I now have a new tool to use with my clients, and hopefully it can also reach many people who aren't my clients. It might even bring me new clients I can work with in person in the San Francisco Bay Area in California, or virtually on Skype.

I've met many great people along the way while conducting my interviews and research, and I'm thankful to them for allowing me to put their experiences in print to help someone else starting on this transition. I've mentioned them on the acknowledgments page.

Most importantly, I've done what I wanted to do every day. I've had the freedom to relax and do nothing, read, walk, ride my bike, see a client, meditate, write my book, take a hike, or get a tooth implant (that was fun).

I work as much as I want to, and feel like I'm helping others transition to retirement and aging, and assisting them in making good choices about how to thrive in the third stage of their lives.

I'm finding new friends and groups of people to collaborate with so we can make changes we all feel passionate about.

There are things I didn't get around to, but that's what next year and all my future years are for.

I miss many of the people I used to work with, and the team I was part of. I've gotten together with some of them, so I still feel connected to what's going on and the company where I used to work. It was an adjustment not going to work every day, and I had to keep myself from checking my phone, texts, and email constantly.

But, I can't say I've missed my full-time corporate job. It was a great experience while I was there, and I was fortunate to have a satisfying career I'm proud of, and a good employer. I gave the company three months notice before leaving, had my successor identified and helped him onboard, my team was in a good place, and our financial results were on target. They gave me great retirement parties and a memory book with pictures of all of us, and many kind messages from team members about the impact I made on them. This process gave me a good sense of closure. But, it was still tough to let go.

Fortunately, there's been so much else to keep me busy this year, and I feel finished with the past stage of my life now, and am on to new things.

I never could have imagined this life a few years ago when I was working nonstop and most of my thoughts were consumed with work. That was satisfying and challenging at the time, but I can honestly say now is the best time of my life so far. I know anything could change at any minute, and as I said before, change is what this stage of life is all about. Whatever the change is, I'll try to make it an advantage as much as possible. This approach won't always be easy, but it depends on my perception and mindset. There are many things I'll have no control over, but I've learned to trust things will work out the way they're supposed to, which may not be the way I want, but is the way it's meant to be.

At 68, I'm now at the beginning of my elder years, and it will be interesting to see how I feel 10 years from now. Maybe I'll write another book when I'm 78, and another when I'm 88 to chronicle how things change from one decade to the next in this third stage of life.

I'm beginning to see a trilogy in my future, when I thought at one point there was no way I was ever going to finish this book!

I can now look forward to my future years, and know there's no need to be fearful about what it means to get older. I'm curious and open to explore the rest of my life. I can do what I want with it. And, I still feel like every night's Friday night.

Acknowledgments

Writing a book is another paradox because it requires opposite activities, all of which I like, but on certain days they drive me crazy. It's a solitary activity requiring long hours at the computer, but you also need to talk to many people, read books, and do research to get a feel for how others approach the topics you're writing about. I couldn't have written this book without all those people who had their own opinions about this third stage of life.

I want to thank the people who agreed to be interviewed and opened their lives to me, even though many had never met me.

In order of chapters, I want to thank Anne G., Trish R., Lita Reyes, Richard R., Steve S., Dr. P., Dr. Dave, Terrie Carpenter, Kathy H., Dick F., Arden H., Kayla C., and Bette.

I asked five people whose opinions I trust to be beta readers and give me their feedback on the manuscript before it went to the editor. Thanks to Kevin Gagan, Terrie Carpenter, Maureen Viano, Diana Sullivan, and Lita Reyes. They all had good comments and they helped me make the book stronger.

Thanks to the company, BookBaby, who helped me self-publish the book. As a first-time author, I didn't want to spend a lot of time trying to find an agent or publisher, and Karen Maneely kept the project on track, as well as their editing and design teams.

I also want to thank all the authors who wrote books I recommended to my readers. I read many books during this process, but the ones I list in the Bibliography influenced me the most.

There would be no book if my husband, Michael Huff, hadn't been saying for years, "You should write a book," and kept everything else in our lives together while I focused on my third stage of life businesses and this book. He's the best.

Until now, I hadn't found a topic that compelled me to take the time and do the research required to write a book until I started working with my clients to help them make the transition from their full-time jobs to retirement and the third stage of their lives. They inspired me to write something that would help them and all the thousands of people who retire every day. I also wanted to offer hope to the younger people whose identities are still totally focused on their work. They tell me they're afraid to retire because, "What would I do with myself?" or "How can I afford to live without my paycheck?" I felt like that three years ago, so thanks to all of them for inspiring me to try to make sense of this transition from working flat out to finding a new way to live that combines life and work in a more satisfying way. We owe it to those coming after us to model a new kind of aging they can look forward to.

Ways to Contact Me

Let me know what you thought of the book, or connect for any reason at andrea@andreahuff.com. You can email me to set up a time to discuss doing coaching with me in person or virtually. You can purchase copies of this book or learn more about my coaching services at my website EveryNightsFridayNight.com.

Bibliography

Amen, Daniel G. M.D. and Tana Amen, BSN, RN. *Brain Warrior's Way*. New York: New American Library, 2016.

Applewhite, Ashton. *This Chair Rocks: A Manifesto Against Ageism*. Networked Books, 2017, revised edition.

Arrien, Angeles. *The Second Half of Life*. Boulder, CO: Sounds True, 2007.

Bacci, Ingrid. *The Art of Effortless Living*. New York: Tarcher Perigree, 2002.

Birsel, Ayse. *Design the Life You Love: A Step-by-Step Guide to Building a Meaningful Future*. Berkeley: Ten Speed Press, 2015.

Burnett, Bill and Dave Evans. *Designing Your Life: How to Build a Well-Lived, Joyful Life*. New York: Alfred A. Knopf, 2016.

Carpenter, Terrie. *Hello, My Name Is Pain*. San Rafael: Terrie Carpenter, 2017.

Carpenter, Terrie. *Gathering Years: How to Grow Old Without Killing Yourself*. San Rafael: Terrie Carpenter, 2017.

Cohen, Darlene. *Turning Suffering Inside Out: A Zen Approach to Living with Physical and Emotional Pain.* Boston: Shambhala Publications, 2002.

Davies, Clair and Amber Davies. *The Trigger Point Therapy Workbook*, Third Edition. Oakland, CA: New Harbinger Publications, 2013.

Dethmer, Jim, Diana Chapman & Kaley Warner Klemp. *The 15 Commitments of Conscious Leadership.* Conscious Leadership Group, 2014.

Dihnugara, Khurshed and Claire Genkai Breeze. *The Challenger Spirit.* New York: LID Publishing, 2011.

Dow, Mike Ph.D. *The Brain Fog Fix.* Carlsbad: Hay House, 2015.

Egoscue, Pete with Roger Gittines. *Pain Free.* New York: Bantam Books, 2000.

Egoscue, Pete with Roger Gittines. *Pain Free Living: The Egoscue Method for Strength, Harmony and Happiness.* New York: Sterling Ethos, 2011.

Esmonde-White, Miranda. *Aging Backwards: Reverse the Aging Process and Look Ten Years Younger in Thirty Minutes a Day.* New York: HarperCollins, 2014.

Hartwig, Melissa and Dallas Hartwig. *The Whole 30.* New York: Houghton Mifflin Harcourt, 2015.

Hitzmann, Sue. *The Melt Method.* New York: HarperCollins, 2013.

Holliday, Ryan. *The Obstacle Is the Way: The Timeless Art of Turning Trials into Triumph.* New York: Portfolio/Penguin, 2014.

Ikeda, Daisaku. *Third Stage of Life: Aging in Contemporary Society.* Santa Monica: World Tribune Press, 2016.

International Living Magazine, January 2017.

Jampolsky, Gerald M.D. and Diane Circincione Ph.D. *Aging with Attitude.* Seattle, WA: CreateSpace, 2016.

Judkins, Rod. *The Art of Creative Thinking.* New York: Penguin Random House, 2016.

Kabat-Zinn, Jon. *Full Catastrophe Living.* New York: Bantam Books, 2013.

Kelley, Tom and David Kelley. *Creative Confidence: Unleashing the Creative Potential Within Us All.* New York: Crown Business, 2013.

Kleon, Austin. *Steal Like an Artist: 10 Things Nobody Told You About Being Creative.* New York: Workman, 2012.

Merchant, Nilofer. *The Power of Onlyness: Make Your Ideas Mighty Enough to Dent the World.* New York: Penguin Random House, 2017.

Nepo, Mark. *The One Life We're Given: Finding the Wisdom That Waits in Your Heart.* New York: Atria Books, 2016.

Newhouse, Meg Ph.D. *Legacies of the Heart.* EBook Bakery Books, 2016.

Perlmutter, David M.D. *Brain Maker.* New York: Little, Brown and Company, 2015.

Perlmutter, David M.D. *Grain Brain.* New York: Little, Brown and Company, 2013.

Pevny, Ron. *Conscious Living, Conscious Aging.* New York: Simon & Schuster, 2014.

Richmond, Lewis. *Aging Is a Spiritual Practice.* New York: Penguin Random House, 2012.

Sadler, William A., and James H. Krefft. *Changing Course: Navigating Life After Fifty.* The Center for Third Age Leadership Press, 2007.

Sangharakshita. *The Three Jewels: The Central Ideals of Buddhism.* Cambridge: Windhorse Publications, 2013.

Schroeder-Saulnier, Deborah. *The Power of Paradox: Harness the Energy of Competing Ideas to Uncover Radically Innovative Solutions.* Pompton Plains: Career Press, 2014.

Schucman, Helen and William Thetford. *A Course in Miracles.* Mill Valley, The Foundation for Inner Peace, 2007.

Tolle, Eckhart. *The Power of Now.* Novato: New World Library, 1999.

Andrea Huff is an expert coach and consultant for people ages 50 plus preparing for an active retirement. She was the founder of the Executive Coaching and Leadership Development Practice for the leading global career and talent development company, Lee Hecht Harrison, where she was also a Managing Director and member of their Executive Team.

In her current coaching practice, she specializes in working with people who are making the transition to the third stage of life.

Her holistic process helps them find the most meaningful ways to use their time, open new businesses or modify current ones, manage their health, be creative, develop inner lives and find new purposes that are satisfying and meaningful.

She takes a fresh look at these topics in a comprehensive and joyful way that offers new thinking and is easy to read. Ms. Huff uses design thinking, prototyping and paradox thinking to put a new spin on ways to discover who you're meant to be at this age. She also covers the downsides of aging, and how to turn change and adversity into an advantage.

Every Night's Friday Night gives you the process and courage to embrace retirement and aging knowing the best is yet to come.